IN SEARCH OF A COMMUNITY'S PAST

THE STORY OF THE
BLACK COMMUNITY OF
TRENTON, NEW JERSEY
1860-1900

Jack Washington

Africa World Press, Inc.
P.O. Box 1892
Trenton, New Jersey 08607

Cover design by Ife Nii Owoo

Book design and electronic typesetting from author's disk
by Malcolm Litchfield
This book is composed in Palatino and Optima Bold

Library of Congress Catalog Card Number: 90-81574

0-86543-164-7   Cloth
0-86543-165-5   Paper

This book is dedicated to
Dawne and Rita Washington
as well as all the students in the
Trenton Public Schools

CONTENTS

PREFACE

I am a history teacher in the Trenton public school system. The population of Trenton is just under 100,000 of which nearly 50 percent is African American. The school district in which I teach is approximately 85 percent African American. As a teacher, I found that I had to develop projects that concern students and their needs.

Quite often, I would discuss Trenton, the American Revolution, and the Civil War. Too often, questions would arise concerning the role played by African Americans in helping to make America the nation it is today. Much of the questioning would center on the local community. Consequently, I found myself trying to answer questions regarding information not covered in the textbook.

I resolved to conduct some basic research on the questions raised by students. To my amazement, there was no book, manuscript, extended article or journal that related the history of the African American community of Trenton, New Jersey. There were numerous books on Trenton by Elenore Shuman, Harry Podmore, and others. These authors detailed a clear picture of Trenton from its earliest days; however, their approach to the African American community was limited to a paragraph or two.

Since Trenton is the capital of the state of New Jersey, I felt that my task would not be a difficult one. I felt surely there are books concerning the African American community. I continued to search. I discovered, however, that no such books were ever written. To this end, I resolved to develop my own manuscript on the African American community of Trenton. I hope this manuscript would be valuable to the teacher in the classroom as well as to the community at large, with a particular audience being the New Jersey African American population.

I began my research by looking at the Census Tract of 1860-1870 and 1880. No census record is available for 1890 due to a fire which destroyed a large portion of those entries. The census, for example, lists names, occupation, place of birth, race, and amount of property owned. This gave me an indication of who lived in Trenton and the types of jobs they held. I then reviewed every city directory for Trenton from 1860-1900.

For the most part, my information was greatly enhanced by reviewing old news articles (e.g., *Daily True American, The Daily State Gazette, Trenton Times, Sunday Times Advertiser, The Sentinel* [an African American newspaper], etc.). The newspapers proved to be an invaluable source of information. Church records and journals enabled me to collect much needed data. Other sources included municipal records and government documents, as well as minutes of the Trenton

Board of Education. To this end I was able to sketch a picture of Trenton and the African American community; yet there still is much to be done.

JACK WASHINGTON, ED.D.

Trenton NJ
May 1990

ACKNOWLEDGEMENTS

The researching and writing of a book is a long, lonely and frustrating experience. Quite often much needed material is unavailable or is limited in scope and quality. Consequently, the writer must prevail upon individuals for support and encouragement. The long hours in research could not have been accomplished were it not for Joanie Bullock and others who early on saw the need for this project. I was greatly supported by Walter Culbreth, a local artist, who often pushed me when it appeared that I would abandon the efforts. Other persons who supported my work include: Bob Lawrence, President of the Trenton Branch of the NAACP, Paul Pintella of the Trenton Urban League, Nathanial Cobb, North 25 Project, Buster Soaries of Shiloh Baptist Church, Wanda Austin, Mr. Omowale, Beverly Jones, Doc Long, all teachers at Trenton High School who understood what I was doing and gave me much needed direction. I am particularly indebted to my supervisor, James Schlimm, who gave me the opportunity to move forward with his advice and motivation. Ernest Jones boosted my desire to complete the project through his genuine concern to see this document reach publication.

There were those people who proved invaluable beyond measure. These people actually worked with the raw product. Sally Lane of the *Trentonian* newspaper read the first draft and gave some very insightful comments, as well as Dr. Joseph Dibiase, Supervisor of Foreign Languages for Trenton Public Schools. I was greatly assisted with information given to my by Robert Lewis, Bob Craig, Gladys Carmichael, Rosa Mae Briggs, and Dr. Lawrence Hogan, Professor of History at Union County College.

Finally, I would be remiss if I did not the mention the staff in the reference department at the Academy Street branch of the Trenton Public Library. The entire staff patiently helped me to conduct the research. Of particular help was Mr. Reeves of the Trentoniana Collections and Mrs. Wright in reference. Tyrone Harvey, Karen Barksdale and Susan Tiller were priceless in their efforts. To all these people I would like to express my appreciation for their time, concern and support. The greater portion of this work was made possible through the works of journalists such as John Cleary, Harry Podmore and Bill Dwyer. Their documents did much to guide my research and for this I am truly grateful.

Trenton's Historical Churches

Union Baptist church

St Paul's AME Zion

Mt. Zion AME Church

Shiloh Baptist Church

Part One

INTRODUCTION

The city of Trenton, located on the banks of the Delaware, fifty-five miles from New York and thirty miles northeast of Philadelphia, in 1860 was home to nearly 18,000 people of which approximately 700 were African American. The early settlers who came to the city helped to add a historic and cultural richness that is still very much a part of the city today; and it was here that George Washington met and defeated the British at the Battle of Trenton. This important triumph set the tone that ultimately lead to the surrender of the British at Yorktown, for it proved to be a major morale booster during the dark days of the revolution. Much of this history of the revolutionary struggle is clearly visible in and around the city. This includes the old barracks, Eagle Tavern, the Douglas House, St. Michael's Church and the old Masonic Lodge.

Trenton served as a platform for such figures as Abraham Lincoln, who addressed the New Jersey

General Assembly while in route to Washington to receive the oath of office as President of the United States (later his funeral train made a stop in Trenton on its way to Springfield); Daniel Webster, who argued the famous Goodyear vs. Day rubber case (1852) which in the final analysis propelled the name Goodyear a quantum leap forward in the rubber manufacturing process, and General George B. (Little Mac) McClellan, who briefly made Trenton his home after being relieved of his command by President Lincoln. McClellan, with the overwhelming support of the city, was later elected governor of New Jersey. It was here that Trenton's new arrivals—German, Irish, Italian, and Jews—brought their skills and cultural diversity.

It is amid a backdrop of rich social, political, and religious history that the African American community arose, for much of the story of the city cannot be told without coming to grips with the contributions made by the African American community who was clearly part of the city but somehow became lost in the pages of history. Consequently, the story of Trenton is incomplete without some clear appraisal of a forgotten element in the historical framework that made the city so important to the nation. In order to bring the history into proper perspective, historians must go in search of a community's past.

The African American Community Before the Civil War: Separate and Apart from the City

Race and class distinctions were apparent in the city of Trenton in 1860 and clearly delineated one's status in life. The affluent gentry was addressed as "Mister" or with Esquire after their names or "Mistress;" the middle class—composed of artisans and farmers—as "Goodman" or "Goodwife;" the lowest class, servants and laborers, by their first names. The lower class included former slaves, most of whom were black, for slavery was legal in New Jersey until 1846 (*Trenton: 300 Years of an American Town*, p. 7).

Trenton was home to nearly 700 blacks who lived mainly in the North Ward. The 1860 census revealed that for the most part these African Americans, who lived on such streets as Higbee, Feeder, Willow and Perry Streets, were relegated to the domestic services. African Americans, including Amos Jones, George Wood, Edward Tillman, Jane Lake, Lisa Williams, Henry Herbert, and Richard Fletcher were either cooks, washer women, waiters, dressmakers or carriage drivers. Most owned little or no property. One exception was Samuel Gould, a teacher in the public schools for African Americans. Gould, who was born in 1822 in Pennsylvania, with his wife Lucy managed to amass $10,000 in real estate and $500.00 in personal wealth. African Americans who lived in Trenton in 1860 were either born in New Jersey, New York, Pennsylvania or Delaware, with a few coming from Maryland. None was born in the Deep South. They were classified as being either black, mulatto or colored, and were forced to live in the old northern section of Trenton, where there were few municipal services.

There was a very rigid color line that divided the races. Segregation was a clear and pronounced way of life. Even Trenton city directories, official business listings, had a separate section listing African American Trentonians. Consequently, community residents who lived in Trenton founded their own institutions which were separate and apart from the white social and political institutions.

Churches Serving Black Trenton

By the 1800s, a number of churches were founded which became the strongest and most enduring institutions for African Americans in Trenton. They included Mt. Zion African Methodist Episcopal Church on Perry Street, St. Paul's on Willow Street, the Berean Baptist Church on Green and Perry Streets, St. John's African Methodist Episcopal Church on Woodruff Street, the Shiloh Baptist Church (then known as the First Colored Church of Trenton), and several other minor storefront churches that had few members. It appears as though the African Methodist Episcopal (AME) and Methodist Episcopal (ME) churches led religious life for most of Trenton's blacks. Most were members of either Mt. Zion or St. Paul's. There were, however, other AMEs such as St. Mark's on Jefferson Street and the small Asbury ME Church on Montgomery Street.

Perhaps the church that did the most to guide the African American community during troubled times was the Mt. Zion AME Church on Perry Street. Mt. Zion was the first African American religious organization in Trenton. It was first known as The Religious Society of Free Africans of the City of Trenton and was incorporated on February 16, 1811. The trustees at that time included James Berry, Julius Steward, Leonard Ennis, Sampson Peters and Francis Miller. The year 1816 marked the first General Conference of the AME. It was at this time that Richard Allen, the founder of the AME Church, came to Trenton and admitted Mt. Zion into the ranks of the AME fellowship. The congregation for many years was known as the Mt. Zion African Church. The present name of the church was adopted on July 18, 1834, under the trustee board, whose members included: Leonard Scott, William Water, Henry Pearson, George B. Cole, John Treyes, George McMullen and Thomas Voorhees. Perhaps the person most instrumental in the early development of Mt. Zion was Sampson Peters, who became the first regular pastor in 1816. Peters, who was a cooper by trade, allowed the church to worship in his cooper shop while the construction of the present site was underway. It was Sampson Peters who led Mt. Zion to become part of the AME denomination. When Richard Allen preached a sermon in Trenton in 1816, he was Peters' personal guest. In 1820, Reverend William Proctor moved the church from the cooper shop to Perry Street. Church records revealed that the church was enlarged by Rev. Caleb Woodyard in 1858. Mt. Zion pastors rarely stayed in one location more than two years. Peters was the only pastor in the 1800s to stay a period of three years. Consequently, from 1816-1900, Mt. Zion had forty-six different pastors.

Much of the membership of Mt. Zion came from the free and upper class African American society. The leaders of the church were scholarly men who, during their brief tenure in the community, took an active role in affairs that affected the African American citizens of Trenton.

Mt. Zion's growth and development was not without some pain, however. In 1852 there was much dissension among the church members about transfer ministers (ministers from outside the state) being brought into the church to serve as pastors. Consequently a sort of home-state rule policy was put in effect. According to the *Sentinel*, this doctrine was known as "Jersey for Jerseymen."

Notwithstanding the growth pains, Mt. Zion became the leading religious institution in the African American community. Few churches stood the test of political, social and religious uncertainty and remained as strong.

Another church that guided the African American community was St. Paul's on Willow Street. The St. Paul's congregation was quite instrumental in the growth of the community, giving help to the poor, food to the hungry and even serving as a schoolhouse for the African American children when the Ringold School was closed to make way for a new school. St. Paul's present building was erected in about 1881. The early history of St. Paul's on Willow Street near Pennington Ave. dates back to 1840. Meetings were held on Allen Street and Reverend Isaac Gassoway was one of its first pastors. Meetings were later held on West Hanover Street, Tucker Street, Broad Street and finally on Willow Street.

Shiloh Baptist was the outgrowth of the Berean Baptist Church, pastored by Rev. C. A. Berry, and was located at 118 Perry Street. The Berean Baptist Church congregation was quite mobile, having set up locations on South Broad Street, the old City Hall building on Broad Street, Hanover Street and the old Fire House on New Willow Street. A brief history of Shiloh appears in the *Inventory of the Church Archives of New Jersey*, prepared by the Historical Records Survey Division of Women's and Professional Projects—Works Progress Administration (1938). This church was first known as Macedonia Baptist Church. The present title was adopted in 1894. The first constituent members were from the disbanded Berean Baptist Church. During the late 1880s services were held in homes of members on Summer and Church Streets, and from 1896 to 1902 in Salvation Army Hall at 118 Perry Street. The Trenton Baptist Association purchased a site for the church at 104 Belvidere Street in 1899. The church was dedicated in 1902. The church was built at its present site in 1916 and dedicated the following year. In 1930, it was enlarged to a two-story red brick structure, with gray sandstone trim, modified Gothic architecture, a square tower and rounded stained glass memorial windows. The large stained glass window in front of church was donated by Baptist Churches of Trenton. Church properties include the former church, now used as a lodge room, the house adjoining it, formerly used as a day nursery, and the sexton's home adjoining the present church. The first resident clergyman was Rev. John Allen. Active organizations in the church at that time were Sunday School, Women's Mission Circle, Gospel Chorus and Settlement Workers. During this period of growth, seven different ministers served the church.

Another church that was an important part of the African American community was Union Baptist on

Pennington Avenue. According to church archives, Union was organized in 1888 and incorporated in 1908. The first members received letters of dismissal from Shiloh Baptist Church. The first church was a small frame structure on Belvidere Street, built in 1898, enlarged in 1901 and rebuilt in 1915. It was sold in 1926. The site for the present church was purchased in 1920. Additional lots were purchased in 1924; the church was built and dedicated in 1926.

That the churches of Trenton became the backbone of African American life is quite an understatement. They provided shelter for the homeless, clothes for the needy, religious refuge for the despairing and leadership for the African American community at large. African American ministers were well received by the total community. The church served as the guide for much social and political reform, even during the earliest period of African American life in Trenton. Another important function of the churches was to provide a place of final rest for many devoted members.

African American Cemeteries

African American cemeteries were set aside for Trenton residents as early as 1802. In April of that year a committee was appointed by the mayor and Mr. John Beatty to acquire a burial place for the African Americans of the city. A tract of land was secured on Brunswick Avenue. The tract, measuring two acres, was purchased from Nathan Beaks around 1804. The area was then known as Gallows Hill. It is believed that it was named Gallows Hill because the area served as a public hanging site for condemned criminals. It later became the site of several ghost stories. People often told stories of unexplained events taking place there. Before the Civil War the area around Brunswick Avenue and Paul Avenue (Gallows Hill) suffered an epidemic of smallpox. A small makeshift hospital was erected in the area. The African American residents who were fatally afflicted were then buried nearby. The small frame hospital was later acquired by John Kelly. The house around the cemetery at the corner of Race Street served as a refuge for tramps, vagrants and prisoners of the city. Kelly provided the African American citizens of Trenton with lodging. Conditions were not the best; in fact, they were deplorable. African Americans who had no money were accommodated if they presented a red ticket (provided by the city) in order to secure a night's lodging. The ticket also provided for breakfast and coffee. The city of Trenton paid Kelly fifteen cents for each ticket issued.

Another place for the interment of African American residents was on East Hanover Street, near the graveyard of the Society of Friends. The original plot was 20 square feet and dated back to the American Revolution. It served as the burial site for slave-holding families in the city.

Mt. Zion AME Church had a small cemetery in the rear of the churchyard. Many of those interred, including the Steward and Henson families, were members of the church. In 1876, the church was renovated by Pastor Rev. V. U. Stevenson. As a result of the renovation efforts, the bodies were removed from the cemetery and placed in the Locust Hill Cemetery at the foot of Hart Avenue in East Trenton. The Locust Hill Cemetery served as the site for Trenton Lager Beer Brewery in the 1850s. German beer was brewed on what later became the cemetery plot of East Trenton.

The Hart Avenue burial ground was another place for the interment of African American residents. Church ground quite frequently served as burial sites and pastors quite often found a place of final rest for members. Other organizations, including the Colored Female Association, sought to purchase tracts of land in the city to serve as burial grounds. Led by Mrs. Percy Hutchins and Mrs. Spencer Emmons, a fair and festival was held at Temperance Hall with the proceeds being used to buy plots of land to serve as cemeteries.

Prior to the 1830s (at this time the Trenton Common Council officially set aside a portion of city land for African Americans), African Americans were buried in common graves that were unmarked and later abandoned. Those graves not abandoned were uprooted to make way for city expansion. Houses and municipal buildings were located on many of the African American cemeteries.

The Princessville Cemetery (set up around 1840 in back of the Methodist Episcopal Church—and later moved to Bakers Basin in 1867) has been reclaimed. This was a white cemetery; however, there are four African American Civil War veterans interred there. They are William Willis, Joseph Canada and his wife Eliza, James Parker, and Robert Que.

Trenton, a Major Route on the Underground Railroad

The atmosphere in Trenton, although segregated and racially prejudiced, must be evaluated in terms of nineteenth century standards. One might conclude that there were few rights and privileges that the African American community enjoyed. From a twentieth century perspective, this is quite true. Nineteenth-century Trenton, however, experienced a sort of benign prejudice that was tolerant of limited African American aspirations. In some areas, the atmosphere appeared to be somewhat progressive, championing such causes as abolitionism to a far greater extent than other similar communities.

The year 1860 was the dawn of a decade that seemed full of promise for America. This new decade would change the course of American history in that it ushered in a new awareness of Americans regarding freedom, equality and justice for a people who had long suffered from the inequality that was inherent in American society. Freedom was on the minds and in the conscience of Americans, both black and white.

This year marked the emergence of a new social order, for slavery had become the central national issue. It was also an election year and the name Abraham Lincoln was beginning to reach the ears of Northern and Southern politicians alike. African Americans had lived in Trenton, New Jersey, since the Revolutionary War and many in the African American community began to wonder whether the tall, thin lawyer from Illinois would be the ultimate savior for their race. After all, he was opposed to the spread of slavery in the new territories. Only time would tell whether or not his position could become such a force as to eradicate the system entirely.

The debate over slavery was not at all new to Trentonians, who had expressed strong feelings on the subject for nearly a century. Trenton was the home of many antislavery activists, and there are indications that abolitionist sentiment was demonstrated in the city in the eighteenth century. As early as 1774, a Trenton Quaker woman freed her slave, stating:

> Know all men by these presents that I Mary Dury of Trenton in the County of Hunterdon, Spinster, do hereby manumit and set absolutely free my Negro man called James aged about 43 years and do fully release and quit all my Right, Title, Claim and Demand whatsoever of and to the said Negro so that from henceforward he shall be deemed adjudged and taken to be a free man to all intents and purposes at this own disposal with out lett, molestation or hindrance of any person or persons whatsoever for ever hereafter.
>
> In witness thereof I have hereto set my hand and seal this sixth day of the tenth month, called October in the year of Our Lord one thousand seven hundred and seventy four.

According to the *True American*, antislavery feelings first crystallized into an abolitionist society in 1786. Four decades later, a highly vocal organization which was based on religious and antislavery conviction was established by followers of Elias Hicks of New York. The organization's members were known as the Hicks-

Hicksites' Meeting House

ites. Elias Hicks broke with fellow Quakers on the issue of slavery and became an itinerant preacher. In 1827 the Hicksites severed all ties with the parent body of Friends. Perhaps the most fierce opponents of slavery, the Hicksites settled in Trenton and traveled from meeting house to meeting house denouncing slavery as an ungodly institution. The Trenton meeting house still stands on Hanover and Montgomery Streets.

Several leading abolitionists visited Trenton to denounce the institution. One such person who was a frequent visitor to Trenton was Lucretia Mott. Mott was a preacher, writer, lecturer and founder of the Female Anti-Slavery Society in 1833. As the Civil War grew closer, antislavery lectures grew more intense. Miss Frances Watkins of Baltimore spoke against the evils of slavery in Temperance Hall (in 1857) as did William Wells Brown, himself a former slave.

Another such person was Enoch Middleton, a wealthy retired Philadelphia merchant. Middleton purchased property in Crosswicks as a place of residence for himself and his family. Shortly after moving into his residence, he set up a secret abolitionist society allowing his property to become a refuge for runaway slaves.

Citizens of Trenton who opposed slavery included Benjamin R. Plumly. Born in Newtown, Pennsylvania, of Quaker background, Plumly was an ardent temperance advocate and a strong abolitionist. He became director of the Trenton Library Association and the Mutual Life Insurance Company. Plumly helped to organize a network of freedom routes that interlocked fourteen northern states. It thrived until 1861, helping

Rev. T.W.L. Roundtree

Graduate of Oxford University in England
and a leader in the African American
community at the turn of the Century.
Roundtree was born to slave parents in
1866 in Georgia.

to win freedom for 75,000 to 100,000 slaves. In 1866 he moved to Galveston, Texas, where he was elected to the Town Council.

Another strong advocate for abolition was Elisha Reeves. Reeves, a Quaker whose house still stands on River Road, made his residence a stopping point for runaway slaves on the underground railroad. There slaves were hidden away from slave catchers. His home became so well known that it became one of the major landmarks relating to the Underground Railroad prior to the Civil War. Reeves was the grandfather of Senator A. Crozer Reeves, late president of the Trenton Times Company.

Plumly, Middleton, and Reeves were just a few of the many Trentonians who helped make the city a major path for runaway slaves on the Underground Railroad. Even before the railroad was established, free blacks raised funds to aid fugitive slaves. Later, escaped slaves were routed through Trenton from Pennsylvania across New Jersey to Staten Island. The railroad's routes included Bordentown, Crosswicks and Allentown to Princeton. At various intervals were stations that harbored runaway slaves not only in the homes of Quakers and Hicksites, but also freed blacks, Wesleyan Methodists and other members of abolition societies. The stations were often identified by letters of the alphabet. Fugitives were kept hidden in cellars, barns and outbuildings.

The city of Trenton was very much identified with the abolitionist movement. The city, because of the presence of spies and Southern agents, rarely served as the slaves' final stopping point, however. Because of Trenton's reputation as a temporary refuge for

escapees, slave catchers from the South were constantly visiting the city to recapture runaways and return
them to Southern masters. As enforcement of the
Fugitive Slave Law of 1850 intensified, the threat of
being returned to slavery was a constant source of
concern to the entire African American community.
The slavecatchers' search occasionally led to tragedy
and the separation of families. William Gordon, for
instance, literally died of fright at the thought of being
returned to slavery, the *Gazette* reported:

> William Gordon, a malatto [*sic*] who has lived for
> several years in the city, died of convulsions last
> Friday morning under peculiar circumstances. Since
> the excitement arose on the subject of the Fugitive
> Slave Law, Gordon has been in a state of much
> alarm. He was probably a fugitive slave and in
> constant fear of being seized at any moment of the
> day or night under that inhuman law and carried
> off immediately from his wife and children.
>
> Last Thursday evening the colored population of
> this town were thrown into some alarm by the
> report that some persons had arrived in Trenton in
> pursuit of a certain fugitive slave. They immediately
> took efficient measures to dispatch the fugitive
> northward. Two of them met Gordon at the corner
> of State and Warren Streets and told them what was
> going on and dispatched him to a certain colored
> man's home in Woodruff Street [now Allen Street]
> on some errand connected with the business. He
> started off running with all his might but when
> near his residence at the corner of Perry and Mont-
> gomery Streets, he fell to the ground in convulsions,
> caused probably by a rush of blood to the head. He

lay in this state till about 2 o'clock when he died.
The deceased was a respectable, orderly and indus-
trious man.

To prevent the return of runaways to their Southern masters, many local residents came together to aid
fugitive slaves. According to a published article in the
October 19, 1850, issue of the *Daily State Gazette*:

> There has been residing in this city for sometime
> past, a fugitive slave who has married and has
> around him a family. Some days ago, it was re-
> ported that a person claiming to be the owner or
> agent of the owner, had arrived in this city, and
> was on the lookout for his prey. In consequence of
> this, the colored people of this city held a meeting,
> raised funds to send the fugitive and his family to
> a land where the man-hunter will no longer trouble
> him.

The hysteria caused by slavecatchers aroused tension within the African American community and
inspired a measure of sympathy from the white community:

> We did not know that there is a fugitive slave in
> Trenton, but if there is, we hope that his friends
> will immediately take measures to have him sent to
> a place of safety for we really fear that here is not
> that place. (*Daily State Gazette*, October 19, 1850)

The Election of 1860

To be sure, there was a great deal of antislavery sentiment in Trenton. Members of the Republican Party fought to secure a measure of justice. Those who endorsed equality for black people were called Black Republicans—people who could not be trusted to guarantee that African Americans, once freed, would not try to seek revenge against their former masters.

Many supporters of the Democratic Party, on the other hand, were very vocal in their support of the South. They believed that the South had the right to govern its own affairs and they viewed abolitionists and anyone sympathetic to the abolitionist cause as people who were not only out to destroy the South but the United States Constitution as well. Their battle cry was "The Constitution As Is," meaning there should be no amendment to the Constitution that would abolish slavery. Leading the charge against freedom for blacks was the *Daily True American*, a major Trenton Democratic paper edited by David Naar. Naar's views on African Americans are well documented in his lectures and editorials, and are noted by historian Clement Price in his book *Freedom Not Too Far Distant*. According to Naar, the African American was to be feared economically and socially since he was "by nature treacherous ... worthless and imbecilic."

These comments were widely circulated through the streets of Trenton as a polarized community prepared for an unavoidable Civil War. Consequently, with John Brown's Antislavery Raid on Harper's Ferry still fresh in the minds of all Americans, Trenton entered the 1860s.

Prior to the election of 1860, both political parties held nominating conventions to choose their standard bearers. The Democratic Party held its state convention at Temperance Hall, on March 28, 1860, to choose representatives for the New Jersey delegation at the Democratic National Convention in Charleston. The convention debated numerous issues; the resolutions showed, however, that slavery was the dominant theme. The convention condemned the Republicans for seeking to divide the union, called for the strict observation of the existing Constitution, advocated that all legislation on the question of slavery should adhere to the Constitution, showed support for home labor, called for punishment of those who, according to the Democrats, counselled violence against slaveholders and called for strict enforcement of the Fugitive Slave Laws. The convention resolved, for instance,

> That the people are now imperatively called upon to decide whether the Union shall be imperilled or preserved; and the Democratic Party declare, that in their opinion, it cannot be preserved by trampling the Constitution under foot; by violating the laws; by deriding and defying the courts; by a miserable appeal to classes, setting one section of the country at variance with another, and begetting throughout the workshops of the north, a bitter prejudice against the rice fields of the south, nor least of all by armed force; but that it is only by a sacred observance of the Constitution in all its parts; by a ready observance to all federal laws, by respect for, and submission to the judicial tribunals; by doing justly

and dealing kindly and equally with all the States;
that the federal government can discharge its duty,
and the union and prosperity of these United States
be preserved ....

The convention was divided between two strong
factions who debated the issue of slavery. One faction
supported Stephen A. Douglas and his plan of popular
sovereignty. The other supported an extremist position
that protected the system of slavery and its eventual
spread throughout the country. Naar, a convention
delegate, preached moderation and sought to work
out a compromise between the two factions.

"Unfortunately," he wrote back, "there are some
men here too thoughtless to be prudent, or too selfish
to consider anything but the advancement of their
own prejudices, but I believe there are not many of
these and I hope they may be overruled by the greater
number who look to the good of the people of this
Union, as a whole, as a paramount object of this
mission here ...." (*Sunday Times Advertiser*, October
23, 1960)

It appeared as though the efforts of Naar and
members of the New Jersey delegation who sought to
arrest any political fallout were unsuccessful in their
endeavors. The convention developed two reports. The
majority report was produced by Southerners who
would support no measure that would challenge the
South's right to own slaves. The minority report called
upon the Congress not to intervene in the slavery
question. The New Jersey delegation signed the minority report. Although Naar was quite sympathetic to
the South and held pro-slavery views himself, he felt

that a tempered compromise measure was needed to carry the election. The concept of popular sovereignty, which said that each state should decide the slavery question for itself, did not exactly please the New Jersey delegation, which was opposed to the convention nominee Douglas; however, Naar supported Douglas in spite of their differences. Unity was called for in an attempt to mend fences.

Full unity remained elusive, however, because when the minority report was adopted by the convention after a series of backroom deals, the convention ended in much tension. The Southern extremists bolted the convention and supported John C. Breckenridge, an avid supporter of slavery nationwide.

The Democratic Party used the issue of slavery to spread the seed of fear and misapprehension:

> Abolition of slavery! Men of the North have you comprehended it? Have you thought of three million Negroes, wild with their freedom, uneducated, unrestrained by any moral perceptions and ideals, led by their passions alone, lazy, vicious, and uncontrollable? Have you thought of the horrors which this exodus from the South would entail upon you—of this mass of Negroes perambulating your country, stealing and murdering as they go, until a war of races sweep them from the face of the American continent? If you have, and prefer such a state of affairs to their being enslaved in the South, a fact with which you have nothing to do and for which you are not responsible, vote for the black Republicans. (*Times and Advertiser*, October 23, 1960)

The Democrats used the election as a platform to call for support of slavery and rebuke all efforts to alter the system. They viewed the South as the victim who was being denied its rights. Democrats theorized that should the South be denied its property rights, this would be the step that would indeed lead to a challenge of the property rights of all men.

"Let the naturalized citizens be warned in time," read one *True American* editorial. "If they aid in depriving the people of the Southern States of their just rights, they may rely that their turn will come next. The defeat of the Democratic Party will be the signal for oppression and injustice throughout the land."

The Republican Platform

The Republican Convention of that same year was far more unified. The New Jersey delegation to the Chicago meeting went with a fierce determination to push William L. Dayton of Trenton for the presidential nomination. (In 1856, Dayton held the distinction of defeating Lincoln for the vice-presidential position on the ticket. He ran with John C. Frémont on the moderately abolitionist Free Soil and Free Men platform.) The efforts of the New Jersey delegation were to no avail, for Lincoln became the Republican Party candidate.

The tariff question became a part of a program which Trenton Republicans offered to the workingman. Republicans promised to protect the American worker from the threat of foreign labor and to guarantee the worker his freedom from the national troubles.

The Republicans, the Trenton segment of that body claimed, were "advocates of the rights of labor.... They demanded that the territories shall be devoted to free labor, that a sound protective tariff shall protect our laborers from foreign competition, and that the public lands shall be given to those settlers who will really live upon them and cultivate them."

These, then, were the three freedoms which the Republicans offered: freedom from competition of foreign labor, freedom from the competition of slave labor, and freedom to own land as settlers in the West.

Of these three, the threat of competition from slave labor, not the tariff, was emphasized most by Republican speakers in Trenton. At a Republican rally before a reported audience of 3,000, one prominent speaker, ex-Governor Reeder of Kansas, linked the tariff, free homestead, and slavery as the major points of difference between the northern laborer and the southern slave. Reeder maintained that these issues were part of the larger question as to "whether this country shall continue to exist as a Republic or be converted to an oligarchy."

Was slavery a greater threat to the northern workingman than competition from foreign labor? More than one Republican seemed to think so. William Bross, editor of the *Chicago Tribune*, also spoke in Trenton. The *Gazette and Republican* was pleased that Bross "spoke at some length, and eloquently, on the slavery question, showing that it was 'the great living issue of the day.'" The paper, in passing, noted that he also spoke on the tariff, homestead bill and "other great measures set forth in the Republican platform." According to one auditor who wrote an indignant letter to the Democratic *True American*, Editor Bross said "the Tariff had nothing to do with the question at issue in the present campaign." Bross reportedly called slavery "the only question now before the country." (*Sunday Times Advertiser*, October 1960)

Thus the election of 1860 clearly demonstrated the gap that existed between the two major political parties. Lincoln's nomination was met with great displeasure from the Democrats, who castigated the Republican Party:

We ask every honest man in this broad land, can any government exist where the people are taught to disregard and reject the Constitution and the Laws? Does not such a state of things inevitably lead to anarchy and overthrow of government? By what right doo [sic] you hold your debts? By law and the decisions of your courts. But the laws and the courts not only guarantee your rights of property, but they throw around your lives the aegis of their protection. Sweep away all constitutions, all laws, all courts, and where is the protection to life and property? Then the law of force prevails—then confusion reigns—then anarchy is supreme—then the strong sinewy arm and the brawny shoulders decide the rights of property and of life—then ruffian violence tears asunder the bands of matrimony, and gloats in its bestial free-love! Do you prefer this state of affairs to the Government you now have? If yea, then vote for the men who scoff at constitutions, reesist [sic] laws, and defy the courts of the country—vote for Abraham Lincoln. If you do not then aid us in putting down the revolutionary ... black Republican Party.

When Lincoln became the nominee of the Republican Party, the delegates (unlike the Democratic delegates) united behind him as their candidate.

Lincoln's election drew the line of demarcation at the Mason-Dixon border; he carried the North only. New Jersey was the only Northern state which did not support him. Consequently Trenton became the focal point of Civil War politics in the state. Political volleys were hurled at the Republican Party by Naar and his pro-Southern Democrats, who savored every opportunity to belittle the Republicans.

"If the success of Lincoln and his 'higher law' party does not lead to actual and immediate rupture of the confederacy, which we trust it will not," another editorial line went, "it must have the most serious and damaging effects upon every branch of commerce, industry and trade in the country." (*Sunday Times Advertiser*, November 6, 1960)

In the larger sense, the Democratic Party had as much at stake and more common interests with the Northern Republicans than it did with its southern Democrats. In the North both parties were in close agreement on the need for a higher tariff. (The tariff question was a troublesome issue between the North and South as early as the election of Andrew Jackson.) The Southern Democrats advocated a lower tariff. The African American community was used by both parties to intimidate the working man in Trenton. Northern Republicans viewed the slave as competition for the laborer and proposed that the degradation of slave labor was a degradation of all labor. According to the *Gazette* and *Republican* (the Republican Party newspaper and the chief rival to the *Daily True Ameri-*

can): "Free labor everywhere would be degraded and considered odious.... All labor was degraded by the Democratic principle that 'the southern Negro' who is represented as a 'person' in Congress should be classed with livestock of a Northern farm yard in order to secure his admission into a territory."

The election of 1860 was cause for black people to feel optimistic about their future and the future of their children, for Abraham Lincoln was not a staunch pro-slavery candidate. While the African American community looked to Lincoln with hope, some segments of the city viewed Lincoln as a threat to the accepted manner in which they felt the nation should be directed.

Lincoln's eventual election to the Presidency was the final straw. On December 20, 1860, the South Carolina legislature voted to secede from the Union. The attack on Fort Sumter in April 1861 set the stage for the long and bloody Civil War, a war where brother often found himself fighting brother and fathers too often found themselves fighting sons.

Like every other community, Trenton was sharply divided. As noted, New Jersey did not support Lincoln. In Mercer County (of which Trenton is the seat), Lincoln carried the vote over a large pro-South minority. The city became a haven for Copperheads—Southern sympathizers in the North—and Southern spies.

Naar served on numerous committees whose sole purpose it seemed was to impede the advancement of the African American community. Locally, he was president of the Trenton School Board (1861-62) where his policy of denial of educational opportunity to the

African American children of Trenton was clear and unrelenting.

As the tension of the war began to engulf the entire nation, Naar pressed the New Jersey legislature to move to prevent African Americans from the South from entering the state. Naar stated:

> If what we read be true, we may look for a considerable increase of the free negro population in the northern states. It is asserted that the Legislature of Virginia and North Carolina contemplate the expulsion, by legislative enactment, of all the free negroes within their limits. The constant efforts of abolition emissaries to poison the minds of that class of persons in Southern States, has rendered them a very dangerous element of society. In the two states named the number of free negroes is estimated at about fifty thousand. These people are to be expelled and their passage paid to the North, where there are so many black Republicans solicitous of their welfare and anxious to elevate them to social and political equality. There are laws in some of the Northern states denying them admission. New Jersey is one of the states where no such law exists. We may therefore look for a considerable accession to our pauper population and a consequent augmentation of the burdens of taxation—to say nothing of an increased peril to her roosts, a frequency of incendiary fires, and a greater insecurity of all species of movable property—all fruits of the benign policy of the Republican Party. (*Daily True American*, November 20, 1860)

Very little was done to appease Naar and the Democrats. The crisis came to a head around 1863. To the pro-South forces, there appeared to be an "abnormal growth of Negro colonization in Trenton," with resulting clashes between the races. The *Daily True American* became obsessed with the idea that African Americans might gain economic control of the city. Naar went a step further blaming the Black Republicans: "Not content with demanding his political and social equality, these abolition radicals are now found openly advocating amalgamation."

To further dramatize this point, the following poem was published by Naar in the *Daily True American* in 1863:

> They come, they come, in multitude
>   Along Ohio's tide
> The "shucking tramp" of their brogans,
>   By Susquehanna's side
> They feel the winter's icy breath
>   The dreary way along
> They are coming, Father Lincoln,
>   About four million strong.
>
> They come, a nation's guest to share
>   Our firesides and our bread.
> They live without the grammar
>   But they'll die unless they're fed.
> We'd rather pray, it's cheaper, and
>   We'll pray both loud and long
> They are coming, Father Abraham,
>   About four million strong.

Come all ye brave philanthropists
   Philanthropesses Fair;
Turn out your seedy hats and coats,
   And skirts the worse for wear;
Hymn books and musty bacon; bring
   The reeking store along
They are coming, Father Abraham,
   About four million strong.

And though the country may be poor
   And labor be oppressed,
And white men starved and die in want,
   You surely will be blessed;
For Fools, in ages yet to come,
   Will sing your praises long
They are coming, Father Abraham,
   About four million strong.

Then take them to your arms, my braves;
   Don't bid them stay away;
The good times surely coming now—
   The long expected day.
Let brother Beecher raise soft
   The banner and the Song;
They are coming, Father Abraham,
   About four million strong.

This racist agitation caused a great fear to grip not
only Trenton but the entire state, so much so that
when the legislature met in January 1863 legislation
was proposed to curb the immigration of Southern
African Americans. The bill was not received well by
the Republicans, who had gained considerable
strength in the legislature. In fact, the Republicans, led

by Assemblyman James M. Scovel of Camden, offered the following mock resolution:

> Whereas recent African travelers have announced that the elephant is multiplying with unexampled rapidity and having overrun Africa they are about to swim to this continent; and since we have all the elephants we want and the danger of an influx of elephants intimidates small children and increases taxation, therefore that a committee of enquiry be appointed with power to send for persons and papers. (*Sunday Times Advertiser*, by John J. Cleary)

The Assembly Judiciary Committee refused to consider the "anti-immigration" bill; however, another version of the measure, entitled an Act to Prevent the Immigration of Negroes and Mulattoes, passed the Assembly 33-20. A provision of this act required African Americans entering the state to be transported to Liberia.

The social and political unrest was a matter of great concern to all segments of the Trenton community. The fears and apprehensions were widespread with rumors abounding daily as to the impending fate of Trenton. Tension and frustration gripped the city with each dispatch that came across the telegraph lines. There was little doubt whom the residents blamed for the problems as this published joke in the *Daily True American* (February 26, 1861) related:

> Why can't Lincoln have his life insured?
> Because no man can make out his policy.

Racist attitudes were never stronger than during the Civil War. The African Americans of Trenton suffered much from the many New Jersey political leaders who supported the South. (In fact, New Jersey was one of the few northern states that held such a pro-southern view and the only state Lincoln lost both in 1860 and 1864.) Despite the community's best efforts to demonstrate its patriotism during the Civil War, many African Americans found themselves subject to violent assaults. According to a report by William Dwyer of the *Sunday Times Advertiser*, on August 27, 1863, an African American couple was attacked by a group of white segregationists. In fact, several cases of this nature had come to the attention of city authorities, with repeated calls to seize the offenders and make amends to the victims.

Trenton Serves as a Camp for the United States Black Troops

Despite the fact that at the onset of the Civil War President Lincoln was opposed to them serving in battle because he felt they were "servile and cowardly," African American soldiers were ultimately permitted to fight. Nationally they distinguished themselves as every bit the equal to their white counterparts.

There were two campgrounds in Trenton, Camp Olden near Olden Avenue which served as the African American camp site and Camp Perrine on the bank of a canal below the Roebling factory which served the white soldiers. Under the provisions of a Presidential Proclamation issued on January 1, 1863, the enrollment

Unnamed "colored" soldiers in Trenton

of African American men in the United States Army
and Navy was authorized. Regimental organizations
were begun and completed in several of the states.
New Jersey, however, never organized any regiments
of African Americans. African American recruits from
New Jersey were forwarded to Philadelphia, Pennsylvania, where the Chief Mustering Officer was instruct-
ed to muster them. Later, these procedures were
modified so that the New Jersey Superintendent of
Recruiting Service could enroll and muster in these
recruits in the state. They were mustered in by the
Provost Marshals of Districts, and were then forwarded to Trenton, transferred to specified depots, and
were then assigned to the different regiments in the
service. The officers received their appointments, were
commissioned directly from the War Department and
were assigned to commands by that department.

Hundreds of African American troops were mustered into the service from Trenton. In 1864, they
fought in such Virginia campaigns as Bermuda Hundred, Wilson's Landing, Drury's Bluff, Deep Bolton,
Chapin Farm, Cabin Point and other points of military
engagement.

Many gave their lives for the preservation of the
Union, even though the African American troops were
paid $7.00 a month and $3.00 for clothing and other
items while their white counterparts received $13.00 a
month and $3.50 for clothing.

African American Men of Trenton Respond to Lincoln's Draft Order

Although nearly 2,000 soldiers from Trenton served as volunteers for service with the Army of the Potomac (from an estimated 18,000 persons), the manpower was not enough to meet the needs of the Union forces. President Lincoln issued an order in March 1863 drafting all able-bodied men into service for the Union cause.

Lincoln's draft order required full compliance from both the African American and white populations. If one were affluent enough, he might buy his way out of serving for $300 payment to the government, or he might pay some other person to serve in his place.

Thousands of whites answered the call throughout the North. Locally, African Americans of Trenton demonstrated their patriotism by answering the draft. Each city was given a quota. John Suydam, James Holmes, Joseph Canada (buried at Princessville Cemetery), George Daily, Amazaiah Bossley, Alfred Seruby, John Tills, Ridley Onquey and Charles Hopkins were among some of the draftees. Draft registration took place at the old Temperance Hall, a popular location for political and social events in Trenton. Many became part of Company B of the Eighth Colored Regiment.

Those African Americans who proved too old to man the front-lines performed services for the Union cause by working the docks and maintaining much needed public works while the war raged on.

Irish Draft Riots

No ethnic group was more against the war and the fighting than the Irish. According to Rudolph Vecoli, author of the *People of New Jersey*, the Irish, as fervent Democrats, were opposed to the war and to all things Republican. The Irish were opposed to emancipation both because of hatred for the African American and because of fears that abolition would bring hordes of competitive African American laborers into the state.

The opposition to the draft caused hysteria and a sense of chaos. This poem published in the *Gazette* and *Republican* demonstrates the antagonism toward Lincoln (March 17, 1865):

No More Drafts

"Good people vote for Abe,
  The Union to restore,
To liberate the Negro
  And to end this cruel war.
We'll have no more conscription,"
  Said the Lincoln men and laughed;
"So vote for Father Abraham,
  If you'd avoid the draft."

"As soon as rebeldona
  Shall hear the glorious news,
Of Abraham's election,
  They'll tremble in their shoes;
They'll throw away their arms,"
  Said the Lincoln men and laughed;
"So vote for Father Abraham,
  If you'd avoid the draft."

"Jeff. David and Bob Lee
  Will go to Mexico,
And Beauregard and Hood will hide
  Themselves in Borneo.
They'll give us their plantations,"
  Said the Lincoln men and laughed;
"So vote for Father Abraham,
  If you'd avoid the draft."

I took them at their word,
  I voted for their man,
And sat up all election night,
  To hear how shoddy ran.
The telegraph did tick
  The Lincoln men all laughed,
And said, "the Copperheads are sick:
  There'll be another draft."

No Copperhead am I.
  But still I felt quite sick,
To think the draft should follow
  My vote for Abe so quick.
I asked the Democrats.
  How is this? and they laughed,
And said, "How are you, conscript?
  You voted for the draft."

The Irish were discriminated against due to their ethnic background. Indeed, in some cases they found themselves receiving treatment that nearly paralleled the repression experienced by African Americans. All across the state of New Jersey, Irish working men responded to the draft by attacking the African American population of Newark and other cities. In New York City the Irish became enraged with hatred once they found that they would bear the brunt of the draft calls. Many reduced the Civil War struggle to the notion that it had become a ploy to free the Negro. Thus this attitude on the part of many Irish culminated in the Irish Riots.

The first drawing of names on Saturday, July 11, 1863, resulted in a list of 1,200 prospective draftees and most of them were Irish. The names appeared in the Sunday papers. On Monday, July 13, Irish working men gathered in sullen crowds near the draft centers instead of reporting to their jobs. When the police attempted to disperse the crowd, the fighting started. It went on for four days. The mob went from one ghetto to another in search of Negroes. They beat and stomped any Negroes encountered on the streets. They shot Negroes. They hanged Negroes.

The New York riots prompted many African Americans in Trenton to seek city protection. Large numbers called on the mayor for help. One resident, Richard Long, committed suicide after he and his family were attacked at their Willow Street home by a rampaging group of white youth. Long, a waiter, had apparently been despondent over the death of his child, and it appeared that the violence against his family helped to precipitate his suicide. Despite such attacks, Trenton was sought as a temporary refuge by African Americans fleeing from New York City before they moved into the countryside.

On April 9, 1865, the Civil War ended. On April 14, 1865, less than a week after Robert E. Lee surrendered to Ulysses S. Grant at Appomattox Courthouse,

Virginia, President Lincoln was assassinated by John Wilkes Booth. Lincoln's death caused much grief across the nation.

The slain President's funeral train made a stop in Trenton on its way to Springfield, Illinois. Large crowds came out to see this "Great Emancipator." Much of the city was in sincere grief. This, no doubt, included the African American community who felt that a true friend was lost with the death of President Lincoln—the last tragic death of the Civil War.

The Civil War's end in some ways served as the point of departure between two worlds, one where white men ruled and another where the emergence of equality was an idea that all had to reckon with. In many respects, the Civil War was the beginning of an era of awareness, reform, and commitment to social and political change. Nationally, the period of Reconstruction focused primarily on the South; however, the issues raised at that time had far-reaching political consequences locally. No sector of the country escaped the ever-increasing demand for change, and Trenton was in a unique position to see the old world give way to new initiatives, for New Jersey appeared to have dual allegiances, one to the Union and another to some manifestations of Southern concerns.

Part Two

THE POLITICS OF EDUCATIONAL CHANGE 1865-1885

The close of the Civil War era marked a turning point for the African American community of Trenton. The community had already begun to grow in size and influence, and its members began to demand services which had previously been denied as a matter of course. One of the first arenas for change was the system of public schools.

Organized education for the African American children of Trenton had been established long before the Civil War. As early as 1801, Trenton, Salem and Burlington had white-run and white-staffed schools for African American children. By 1809, the Sabbath School was established for African Americans by the Society of Friends. Classes were held in a two-story brick structure known alternatively as the African School House and Jackson Hall. This building, on East

41

Hanover Street near the African American burial grounds, also functioned as a community center.

Although education was required by law from as far back as 1788, no formal public schools existed for African American or white children in Trenton until implementation of the 1824 Common School Law. In 1844, the Common Council set up the present Trenton public schools, with Dr. Charles Skelton as the first superintendent. By this time, a regular budget item of the council was in place for African American education. In spite of these allocations, Jackson Hall fell into disrepair and soon became known as "Nightmare Hall."

African American children were required to pay tuition: "For spelling and reading, $1.00. For these [sic] with writing, arithmetic and geography, $1.25; For these with higher brooches, $1.75."

Although the school was limited in resources (by 1848 children were no longer required to pay tuition—consequently Nightmare Hall was made a free school that was open to all children), it made excellent progress. According to a reporter for the *Daily State Gazette* who visited the school:

> By invitation from the superintendent of the public schools in this city, we visited the colored public school yesterday, in Hanover Street. We confess we were surprised at the order which prevailed, and at the proficiency shown by the pupils—especially in geography, reading and writing. The teacher is a colored woman, and seems to be admirable suited for the position she occupies.

From about 1853 to the summer of 1855, Theodore Doughtry Miller was the teacher. He was popular and during his time here he promoted some cultural activities in the school.

An advance notice of a dramatic entertainment with which Miller was identified is reproduced here from the *Gazette*, January 3, 1855:

> Dramatic—A grand dramatic entertainment is advertised to come off at Temperance Hall this evening. The drama, entitled "The Drunkard," will be played with a full cast of characters, composed of the members of the Metropolitan Association under the supervision of Mr. Theodore D. Miller, teacher of the free school for colored children of this city.

It was in 1855 that the old schoolhouse on Hanover Street was removed from its site. Its demolition came as the result of many complaints regarding its condition. On October 1, 1855, Nightmare Hall was sold at public auction and within ten days was demolished. According to the *Gazette*:

> Nightmare Hall was yesterday knocked down by the auctioneer's hammer for $21. It will now be removed from its present site, and will probably be reproduced on some other lot, fenced in and white washed, and so changed in appearance that none of its present admirers will be able to recognize it. We hope never to look upon its face again.

The demolition left sixty-three African American children without a schoolhouse. With the close and demolition of Jackson Hall and the need to educate the children becoming a major concern, the community agitated the Trenton School Board and the Common Council to set up a school for the African American children.

A School Committee to the Colored School was organized to review the matter. The members included Gearhart, Harris, Taylor and old Judge Yard, among others. A proposal was made to rent a schoolhouse on Washington Street that was owned by John Hazzard. The building would be rented for six months while the school board sought a permanent location. The board also hired A. L. Stanford (1855) to teach the children:

> School For Colored Children—The school trustees have procured a building on Belvidere Street, near Willow, where they have established a school for colored children, under the direction of Mr. Stanford.
>
> He is said to be an excellent teacher, and our colored population have now an opportunity to secure for their children a good education free of cost. As yet the school is small but as it becomes better known it will no doubt increase in numbers and usefulness.

The following year, a teacher was selected from Greenwitch, South Jersey. At this time (1856-57) the African American community north of Feeder Street sent twenty-three males and twenty females between five and ten years of age and twenty-nine males and twenty-two females between the ages of ten and sixteen (total ninety-four) to school.

Higbee or Nixon School

**Teachers in the Trenton Public African American Schools
1844-1874**

Name	School	Position	Salary	Appointed	Retired
Armstrong, Sarah		In charge		Dec. 23, 1850; Sep. 1868	d. 1869
Conover, Ida B.				Jan. 1866	
Dennis, Serene E. B.	Ringold St.		$650 (1876)	May 1874	
Gould, Samuel			$250 (1860)	1858	
Howard, M. A.				Sep. 1869	Oct. 1872
Kasten, Sarah K.	Ringold St.	1st & 2nd grades	$500 (1876)	Jan. 1873	
Miller, Theodore D.			$250 (1853)		Mar. 1854
Shreve, George				1850	
Stanford, A. L.		Principal		Sep. 1855	
Tyrell, M. A.	Belvidere St.			Apr. 1865	Jan. 1866
Wellington, Sarah				Oct. 1867	

The community agitation paid off and in 1857 a new school was erected on Higbee Street (today Bellevue Avenue) for the sole purpose of educating the African American children. The Higbee School (which still stands at 20 Bellevue Avenue) was a two-story brick building (remodelled in 1913).

The Higbee School was constructed to provide a general and basic education for the African American community; however, its educational program did not go beyond the fifth grade. It was a general education curriculum.

It is important to note that there was no high school at this time. The first high school was established in 1874 and did not accommodate the African American population of the city.

As time passed, the Higbee School also fell into disrepair. The growing African American community needed more school space and the Higbee School needed renovations. In 1872 the children were transferred to a rented building on Belvidere Street while a new school, the Ringold Street School, was being built on Ringold Street, and Higbee School was being renovated. Upon completion, Higbee Street School was used as a school for whites and was therefore referred to as the Bellevue Avenue School.

In March 1872 Superintendent of Schools Dr. C. Shepherd dedicated the new school on Ringold Street. The building was a brick structure. The ceremony surrounding the Ringold Street School was elaborate, with leading figures of both the African American and white communities expressing the desire to see equal educational opportunities for the races. Supt. Shepherd said:

> We have a fine two-story building with two rooms. There is nothing superfluous about it, It [sic] is a plain substantial edifice—put up to meet the wants of the children of colored people, for whose Especial Accommodation it has been erected. Here all

Year	Total	Native-Born	Foreign-Born	African American
1800	1,648			
1810	3,002			435[a]
1820	3,492			600[a]
1830	3,925			612[a]
1840	4,035			441[a]
1850	6,461			526[a]
1860	17,228[b]			675
1870	22,874	17,855	5,019	805
1880	29,910	24,191	5,719	1,376
1890	57,458[b]	43,410	14,048	1,732
1900	73,307	56,514	16,793	2,158
1910	96,815	67,888	26,310	2,581

[a] African American includes 181 slaves in 1810, 85 in 1820, 20 in 1830, 4 in 1840, and 1 in 1850. The African American inhabitants are included in the total for each year.
[b] The large increase in population since the preceding decade was due mainly to the annexation of outlying sections.

can go, and here it is to be hoped there will be taught many children who will become honored and respected citizens. It has been the desire of the school board to afford to the colored children the same privileges in respect to education that are enjoyed by white children.

Old Judge Yard remarked: "Train up a child in the way he should go, and when he is old he will not depart from it." Mansfield Herbert "alluded to the early struggles of his race, amidst all their disabilities." Herbert was a community leader whose family had a long and respectable reputation dating back before the Civil War.

Public education at this time was not a right, but a privilege. Students did not merely enroll in school. Applications had to be made to the school board and permits were issued. According to Supt. Shepherd:

> There were 6,000 children in Trenton (1872) while only 2,500 were entered on the school rolls and out of this number, between 1,700 and 1,800 attended school.

The Ringold School had a waiting list of 200 permits for admission.

To suggest that the Ringold School was inadequate to meet the needs of the African American children is an understatement. It was faced with overcrowded classrooms, poorly equipped facilities and inferior materials. By 1879 the committee on school conditions noted dismal conditions:

> The cellar is damp—cellar walls damp and cellar is dirty—Hydrant in ante-room leaks—and room wet and filthy—a small pipe wanted from hydrant to drain heated by stove in cold weather—burn one side, freeze the other. Ventilation fair from window. Thermometer in one room only. Drainage deficient. Outhouse abominably filthy. Too much rail cars drilling and steam whistles.

The community demanded that the school be repaired, renovated or demolished.

It was also at this time that some members of the community thought of enrolling their children in the white schools, which were not much better, but in some cases were at least closer. The African American children at this time were not allowed to attend white schools that might be near their neighborhoods. They had to attend Ringold Street no matter in which part of the city they lived. Some students were forced to walk past half a dozen white schools to get to Ringold Street.

In 1879 a matter came before the Trenton School Board regarding the admission of an African American child to the all-white Market Street School. Dr. Wollman, member of the board, stated that:

> A taxpayer residing in the fourth ward called on him and said that he had applied to the superintendent for a permit for his children to attend the Market Street School and was told that the permits could not be granted.

He brought the matter before the board to determine what prevented the admission of these children to the schools, as Rule Number 17 required the pupils to attend the school nearest to their homes. Dr. Shepherd stated that the Ringold School was built expressly for African American children and that if one person should be allowed to send his children to the white school nearest to which he resided, all the African Americans would claim the right to a like privilege. The permit was denied. This denial of admission did not stem the tide of agitation for better school conditions, however; in truth it was just the beginning.

Political conditions began to change in the early 1880s. Members of the community began to flex their political and economic muscle and Ringold Street School came under greater political assault:

> The question of providing decent and adequate educational advantages for children who are slightly off color, as it were, will have to be solved in a different manner from this (Ringold School). As it is no black man can give his child even a half-way education at the public expense, no matter how much tax he may pay, nor how respectable he may be. (*Sentinel*, October 1880)

Thus members of the African American community began to organize themselves and marshall their political strength. Led by R. Henri Herbert, son of Mansfield Herbert and a leading figure in the black community, they challenged the political structure to abolish the dual system that served both races separately—and to move towards a desegregated district. Herbert skillfully maneuvered not only the African American community but the white community as well, through his editorials in the *Sentinel*, an African American newspaper published between 1880-1883.

Herbert was quite instrumental in getting the New Jersey State Assembly to introduce legislation that would desegregate the public schools in New Jersey. The bill was introduced by two Republican Senators, Francis of Essex County (Newark) and Charles Youngblood of Morris County. The Republicans at this time

(1880-1881) had captured control of the State House with the support of the African American community.

The Bill (Senate Measure No. 209) received full support from Herbert, the *Sentinel* and the Republican machine in Trenton and throughout the state. The *Sentinel* stated:

> Probably no measure more in accordance with the genius of progressive American ideas, more important in its bearing upon the future citizens of this State—especially those of other than white parentage—more just and equitable in its provisions, more righteous in its aim, than Senate bill No. 209, (elsewhere printed in full) introduced and pressed to a successful issue in the Senate this week by Senator Youngblood, of Morris County.
>
> It confers no special privileges upon any class; it guarantees to every child in this State the rights to which it is entitled under the Constitution of the United States and the Constitution of the State of New Jersey, of part of which a large number have for years been illegally deprived—the right of equal educational advantages.
>
> It is a measure, in the success of which every parent, every fair-minded man, but more especially every colored man, is deeply and particularly interested. No matter how poor, nor how humble, nor how black he may be, it will enable him to give his child the same free school education that is given the child of the wealthiest citizen of the State.
>
> The one inestimable privilege, the one great right which the State of New Jersey has always denied to the colored people within her borders, is this right of equal participation in the educational advantages enjoyed by every other class of her

citizens. And it is the great need of the colored people. Education is the mighty river which makes the great sea of intellectuality; the great molding power, the controlling agency in establishing a true civilization. (*Sentinel*, March 12, 1881)

The bill that was finally approved by both houses stated:

A Supplement to an act entitled "An act to establish a system of public instruction" (Revision), approved March twenty-seventh, one thousand and eight hundred and seventy-four.

1. BE IT ENACTED by the Senate and General Assembly of the State of New Jersey, That no child, between the age of five and eighteen years of age, shall be excluded from any public school in this state on account of his or her religion, nationality or color.

2. AND BE IT ENACTED, That any member of any board of trustees of any school district, or any member of any board of education in this state, who shall vote to exclude from any public school in this state, any child between the age of five and eighteen, on account of his or her religion, nationality or color, shall be deemed guilty of a misdemeanor, and on conviction thereof shall be punished by a fine of not less than fifty dollars nor more than two hundred and fifty dollars, or by imprisonment in the country jail, penitentiary or workhouse not less than thirty days or more than six months, or both fine and imprisonment may be imposed, in the discretion of the court.

3. AND BE IT ENACTED, That this act shall take effect immediately.

The full thrust of the Youngblood bill was quite significant. The primary strategy was to gain access to the all-white Trenton High School which barred African American students.

> In the event of its passage we prophesy that some little attention will be paid to the illegal resolution offered by Mr. Henry Mayer, and passed by our own School Board, which provides that the Superintendent shall issue permits to colored children to attend the colored schools only. Thus debarring every child with a drop of other than Caucasian blood in its veins from the privilege of a high school education. (*Sentinel*, March 1881)

To be sure, the Youngblood bill created a great furor among Democrats as well as Republicans:

> Mr. Van Cleef (Dem. Middlesex) moved its indefinite postponement.
>
> Mr. Bonsall (Rep. Camden) spoke against the bill because it will create an agitation which we are trying to prevent.
>
> Mr. O'Conner (Dem. Essex) said it was a just and liberal measure, and should pass, and Mr. Williams said that no man should put himself on record against it.
>
> Mr. Lufburrow (Rep. Monmouth) offered an amendment providing that county and city superintendents shall set off schools for the exclusive use of colored children, when there is a sufficient number to do so.
>
> Mr. Munn (Rep. Essex) characterized the amendment as monstrous, and after some debate it was defeated.

Mr. O'Conner moved the suspension of the rules that the bill might be put on its final passage. Agreed to.

In explaining his vote, Mr. Murphy (Dem. Monmouth) said that Monmouth county desired separate schools, that Fair Haven desired them, and the newspapers were all wrong in their reports on that subject.

Mr. O'Conner said that he would not stultify himself by not voting for the bill after spending the four best years of his life fighting for freedom.

Mr. Wright (Rep. Essex) said he would be ashamed of himself if he voted against the bill.

The measure was summed up on the pages of the *Sentinel* as follows:

The passage of Senator Youngblood's just and righteous educational bill by both houses of the Legislature is an act of which New Jersey may well be proud. It is a measure exactly in accord with the spirit of the times, and is a just recognition of the equality before the law of all our citizens. It gives us in reality *free, public* schools. It removes the greatest bar to the enjoyment of equal opportunities of advancement by all classes. It says that in her public school system, New Jersey knows no race, no religion, no nationality, no color. All are entitled to equal participation in the benefits derived from a common fund, to which all contribute.

And it should be so—it must be so. There can be no unequal citizenship, no half-way freedom.

Questions of social equality settle themselves. No man brings into his social circle those who are distasteful to him, and no law can make him do it.

But the state cannot afford to make a favored class—to recognize distinctions of race, or nationality, or color. And the state, by an overwhelming majority of its Legislature, has decided that in its common schools, it will not do it.

It is something upon which the colored people especially may justly felicitate themselves. It is the greatest stroke of good fortune which has fell [sic] upon them in this state, since the passage of the Fifteenth Amendment. It gives them opportunities for development that they have never before enjoyed.

The bill which passed (largely through Republican support) was voted on 37 to 18. This was a tremendous feat even with Republican support, for the African American community was still viewed as a docile and simple people who would not appreciate education.

The Youngblood legislation proved to be a toothless tiger. The Trenton School Board gave every impression that it would comply with the law. The board admitted two African American children, daughters of John Walser, to the previously all-white Centre Street School in their neighborhood. According to school officials, they were "light complexioned, well behaved and in every way unobjectionable." The admission of the Walser children, however, was nothing more than a token compliance.

African American children of Trenton were now legally allowed to attend the new Trenton High School on Mercer Street (erected in 1874). Shortly thereafter, problems arose when special classes of African American pupils were formed and given specific time periods that were available to them to use the swimming pool. In the meantime, the Trenton School Board lost the legal right to separate the children on the basis of race (M.T.W. 187).

Prior to passage of Senate Bill 209 (1881), there was much interest within the African American community to build another school, perhaps in South Trenton. A special committee was appointed by the trustees to investigate the possibility. The committee as a whole reported in favor of a new African American school; however, committee members Ellis, Meyer and MacKenzie opposed the plan, which was defeated.

After passage of Senate Bill 209, all opposition to the new African American school seemed to have vanished and a committee was set up to locate a site for the new school. Leaders within the African American community proposed several locations; however, Bellevue Avenue was chosen as the site for the new school which did not please Herbert:

> The site on Bellevue Avenue selected for the colored school house is not altogether satisfactory. The neighborhood is said to be of a character that closely approaches unsavoriness, and the location is far removed from the portion of the city in which great numbers of the children live.

When the power structure decided on the Bellevue Avenue location, however, the African American community, many who were perhaps disillusioned, disappointed and politically exhausted, accepted it as a foregone conclusion. In 1883 the Ringold Street School was closed and went back to the city of Trenton. It was later sold for $2,400, and the monies were returned to the city treasury.

The Bellevue Avenue Colored School

The new school for the African American children, which was purchased for $1,125.00 and located on Bellevue Avenue (this structure still stands and is now the David Lodge of Prince Hall Masons), was opened in 1883. Spencer P. Irwin was hired as the first principal at a salary of $800 per year. Miss Ida Herbert taught first and second grades at a salary of $450 per year. The school grade levels were first through the fifth. The building was a four-room structure which seated about 142 students.

Now there were two schools on Bellevue Avenue, one which served the African American children and the Higbee Street School (now called the Bellevue Avenue School since Higbee Street was changed to Bellevue Avenue) which served the white community. As overcrowded classrooms proved to be intolerable, the school board merely added additional rooms to the existing structure of the Bellevue Avenue Colored School.

After a time, new problems arose which were centered around the African American school. There were two schools on Bellevue Avenue with the same name. One was the Bellevue Avenue Colored School and the other was the Bellevue Avenue white (old Higbee) school. The only way to distinguish one from the other was to refer to each as being either the "colored school" or the "white school." Consequently, leaders in the African American community felt that their children were being stigmatized by having their race demonstrated as public evidence of inferiority. In 1891, community leaders urged the school board to rename the African American school. A committee urged that the Bellevue Avenue Colored School be renamed the Frederick Douglass School after the African American abolitionist. The board, however, rejected Frederick Douglass as a name and compromised by renaming the Bellevue Avenue Colored School the Lincoln School. It was also about this time that the Bellevue Avenue Colored School—or the Lincoln School—because of its need to ease overcrowding, added additional rooms and staff. The staff at this time included S. P. Irwin, Principal; Misses Adele Gordon, Ida Herbert, Martha E. Lewis, teachers; Eli James, janitor; and Peter Perrine, assistant janitor.

The Bellevue Avenue Colored School served as the schoolhouse for the African American community up until 1923 when the New Lincoln School (Junior 5) was built. Thus education in Trenton's African American community was a long and hard-fought quest for equality of opportunity. The system remained segregated and unequal until 1944, when legal barriers to segregation were successfully challenged.

Part Three

THE AFRICAN AMERICAN COMMUNITY OF TRENTON DURING RECONSTRUCTION

1865 an Election Year

The election of 1865 was a period of great political contrast between the Democrats and the Republicans and a test of strength between the Northern and Southern positions.

The Democrats called for white supremacy by way of a conservative legislature. The major question placed before voters was whether African Americans should be allowed to vote. "Let there be a grand turnout of all who are opposed to placing the Negro on an equality with the white man," the *Daily True American* advised. The issue of race clearly outdistanced any local concern of the day as Democrats

61

urged the citizenry to: "Rally in your might! Do not let your children and your children's children have to say of you that you disgraced them."

The period immediately following the Civil War was known as Reconstruction. The African American community of Trenton was socially segregated, politically disfranchised, and economically depressed. Reconstruction was a vague notion that meant change was in the making. The period had aroused a spirit of protest within the African American community, for to them emancipation meant eventual universal suffrage for all men regardless of race, creed, or color.

The Negro Suffrage Convention of 1867

As the call for suffrage for African Americans grew, the African American community of Trenton moved to hold a political convention specifically to deal with this and related issues. The community hosted a statewide meeting to set a new course for New Jersey's African Americans.

The gathering was an outgrowth of a great upsurge in political awareness that had engulfed the state. In Bordentown, right next door to Trenton, the African American suffrage movement held a citywide meeting in a billiard hall at the Bodine Hotel. In attendance were people from Trenton who endorsed the idea of a statewide convention and elected five delegates to the Negro State Convention.

This convention was ultimately backed by the Republican State Committee, which had originally planned to meet in Trenton to set up strategy for the upcoming election. (It was unclear if there would be any African American representation at the convention save token remarks by a few African American participants.)

The main thrust of the convention was centered on the right to vote. Leaders of the African American community met at Taylor Hall, with much discussion and many resolutions. The convention unanimously adopted the following resolutions:

> *Resolved*, That the equality of all men before the law without distinction of race or color, is recognized by the early doctrines of the Republic, the Declaration of Independence, the Constitution, the Ordinance of 1787, and the political writings of Washington, Jefferson, and others of the founders, and was sanctioned by the Constitution of New Jersey, formed by the true men of the revolution, that render the plausibly apparent necessity of tolerating slavery by a State right, we have grievously departed from that standard; and that the insertion of the word "white" in the Constitution of 1844 was a violation of the true principles of Republican Government.
>
> *Resolved*, That pledging ourselves to the eradication of the word white from the Constitution of New Jersey by every legal and honorable means, we also call upon Congress to take measures to induce or compel all the States of the Union to establish a just and uniform rule of suffrage, excluding all distinction of class and race or color, so that the citizens of each State shall be entitled to all privileges and immunities of citizens in the several States; and the United States shall redeem its original

promise "to guarantee to every State in the Union a republican form of government."

Resolved, That this doctrine of the absolute equality of all men before the law, of which impartial suffrage is a necessary corollary, is in strict accordance with that sublime declaration of the fathers of the Republic, that all men are created equal, which was and is the corner stone of all our Democratic institutions.

Resolved, That by our action this day, we intend heartily to endorse the votes of our Senators and Representatives in Congress in favor of securing impartial suffrage to all the people of the States lately in rebellion, and to repudiate the charge that we are willing to impose upon others a fundamental principle of government which we are not prepared to accept for ourselves.

Resolved, That the Republican Party of New Jersey, encouraged by past triumph, and proud of the high record of its executive, its Legislatures and its Senators and Representatives in Congress, cheerfully accept the issue of impartial suffrage, as one of the most important questions to be adjusted in the approaching campaign. Confident that it will be sustained by the calm judgment and patriotic sentiment of the people of the State, and the gracious approval of Almighty God.

Resolved, That this Convention approves the course of the loyal majority in Congress in steadfastly resisting the attempts of the President to substitute his will for the authority of Congress in reconstructing the States lately in rebellion, and that we adjure them, as they value liberty and the safety of the nation to persevere in that resistance to the end.

General Robeson read a letter from Governor Ward, acknowledging his acceptance of the invitation to be present and approving of African American suffrage. The governor said:

> Suffrage should be regarded as the inherent right of all who bear the burdens and fight the battles of the nation. Honor, justice and policy alike demand that we should confer upon a long proscribed and injured race, the only boon under which they can maintain and defend their rights. I have no question but that the policy which we regard as necessary for the reconstructed States *will be good for the loyal States*. To do right and to act justly are duties which cannot be limited in their operation by the *boundaries of States and nations*! (*Daily State Gazette*, July 1867)

The Negro Suffrage Convention of 1867 aroused great concern within the white community. Many whites feared the African American vote would destroy the white community, leading to race mixing and African Americans attending white schools on equal terms with white children. These anti-suffrage forces felt that the Republicans were the force behind the demand for suffrage. Consequently, many in the white population resolved to oust the Republicans in favor of the Democrats, who promised to keep the African American community in its place. The leading force driving for the defeat of the Republicans was the *Daily True American* which ran articles on Election Day such as the following: "Vote against taxes to support Negroes in idleness." The paper stated that such a Republican victory would not only mean "unconditional Negro suffrage but also Negro magistrates, Negro jurors, policemen and legislators." (William Dwyer, *Trenton Bygone Days, Sunday Times Advertiser*, Nov. 10, 1967).

> Without prejudice to the colored race, we think all will agree that the Negroes are entirely unsafe for government. . . . We ask attention to the proceedings in another column and we think the people will agree with us the thing [right to vote] is entirely unpracticable. We are willing to go before the people of this state on two questions. We are satisfied that the people of the old and reliable State of New Jersey are not prepared to give to Negroes the right to hold office or to be elected to represent white people in any situation. Voting is a political right, and we are satisfied that it ought not to be granted to the colored population at this time and so think a vast majority of the people of this state. (*Daily True American*, July 24, 1867)

The Democratic Party rallied conservative opinion against the African American vote as courting political and social disaster.

Democrats belittled the "Convention of Culled Pussons" as a strategy that would undoubtedly defeat the Republican Party throughout the state. They concluded that the people were being deceived into supporting the Republican Party and that they would take the earliest opportunity to throw off the incubus and return to their old Democratic allegiance.

The Democrats not only trounced the Republicans locally but managed to gain control of the State House as well. Prior to the election of 1867, the Republicans dominated the Senate 13-8 and the Assembly 33-27. However, the election of 1867 saw a reversal of political control. The Democrats now controlled the Senate 11-10 and the Assembly 46-14.

Clearly, race was the key factor in the demise of the Republican Party, for the Republicans were advocates for a constituent base that had not yet been granted the right to vote. As the Democratic Party changed leadership within the city, the following principles were affirmed:

We believe the Constitution of the United States presents the best form of government for the control of diverse and distinct political communities, ever developed by man, and that its largest benefits can only be enjoyed by the citizen when *all* its provisions are most sacredly and strictly construed and administered.

We believe that the powers of Congress are limited by the Constitution, and that when these limitations are discarded, the citizen suffers in his estate, person and property, and that tumults and disorders follow.

We believe that the great Civil War was a calamity, but that the disrespect manifested for the Constitution by the Radicals, is a still greater calamity, and the real source of all our woe.

We believe in, and shall advocate free speech, a free press, the rights of trial by jury, the privileges of the habeas corpus, and, in short, every right guaranteed by the supreme law of the land.

We believe that the Southern states are entitled to immediate representation in Congress, and too without any other condition or restraint than is imposed on the Northern states; that all representatives therefrom duly qualified, should be at once admitted, and that the deprivation of this right is cruelty to them, and burdensome to us, obliging us to submit to unjust taxation, whilst the means of national prosperity, the true source of revenue, is entirely withheld from them.

We believe that the Freedmens Bureau is an accursed thing, not only the parent of sloth, idleness and vagrancy, but also of crime; it subjects hardworking and overburdened white men to heavy taxation for the benefit of the black man, without the slightest recompense. It is not only without precedent, but in total violation of every principle of government known to our fathers. We therefore denounce it, to be a disgrace to our national character.

We denounce the interference of Congress with the rights of the State, and say that by investing the negroes of the Southern States with the right to exercise the elective franchise, they were guilty of a gross usurpation, for which no rebuke from the people can possibly be too strong. If Congress can thus dictate upon the gravest of all questions, what remains to the people of their respective State governments? If this legislation flow from any power granted, then the function exercised by the State governments can only by styled privileges, not rights ....

We are opposed to extending the right to vote to the negro in New Jersey, because the negro will not, and cannot be benefitted thereby, neither will the white man, because that step being taken, we will be at once on the broad way to amalgamation. The man who is my peer at the ballot box is my peer everywhere; if he may vote for a judge, he can be a judge; if he can vote for a Congressman, he may be a Congressman. The voter can be voted for. (*Daily True American*, July 1867)

It is historically impossible to measure the impact that the 1867 Colored Convention of New Jersey had upon the nation's conscience; however, the realization of its efforts was clear. Enough momentum had been gathered nationally that the adoption of the Fifteenth Amendment, which granted African American men the right to vote, proved to be the most far-reaching of any of the Reconstruction amendments.

By the 1870s the African American population had not made much economic progress. Many were still essentially laborers and domestics. Politically, however, the community was beginning to make its presence felt. Reconstruction in the larger sense had its political impact in the South, the target being the Confederate states. One might suppose that the Southern political example may have influenced the thinking of the African Americans of Trenton who read of Blanche K. Bruce, Hiram Revels, Robert Smalls, and John R. Lynch.

Reconstruction held a political significance. Although Trenton was a Northern city and was firmly entrenched in Northern values, there was much in Trenton that could easily be associated with a Southern philosophy, for just as African Americans could not vote in Georgia, they were also unable to vote in Trenton. The Fourteenth and Fifteenth Amendments were of particular importance, for these amendments underscored basic rights for both Northern and Southern African Americans. The Fifteenth Amendment had the greatest initial impact of all the Reconstruction amendments for its thrust was immediately recognized by the African American citizenry.

With the ratification of the Fifteenth Amendment came the right to vote and to influence the political system. The African American community felt that its time had finally arrived, and there was a great celebration in Trenton.

The *Daily True American* reported:

> Early in the morning the citizens of African descent were bustling, and about nine o'clock the Delmonico colored band arrived from Philadelphia and played down to Taylor Opera House. A colored band was also present from another part. Colored men, in uniform, dashed hither and thither, and many of sable hue on horseback, with the word "Marshal" round their hats, galloped about the streets. Teams brought in a large number of colored people from the country. Colored women on the streets were numerous, decked in their Sunday-go-to-meeting clothes. Colored children partook of the excitement of the holiday, and by eleven o'clock while citizens were out in large numbers to see what was to be the order of the day.

The Republican leaders who openly sought African American support prepared for the election of 1870—the first election in which the African American was legally able to cast a vote. To the Republican's surprise, about forty African American Trentonians appeared to take part in the meeting as a full partner. They expected to have the right to run for office with the full support and backing of the Republican machine. To their chagrin, the African Americans were rebuffed and denied admission entirely; the Republicans had not imagined that the African American would seek to represent himself. The regular Republican leadership felt that it would "manage" the African American vote while serving as a benevolent guardian over what it saw as a curious but ever grateful people who could do no better than to have Republicans as their friends.

To the credit of some Radical Republicans, there was some discussion about nominating a candidate from the Fifth Ward for a seat on the Council. His name was Anthony Fisher, a mulatto, 52 years of age and the father of seven children. Fisher, who worked as a hotel waiter and a whitewasher, lived in the Fifth Ward. Not much support was forthcoming from the Republican leadership, who hand-picked nominees for office, and Fisher's nomination was rejected.

The meeting so angered the African American community that Fisher decided he would run for office himself with or without the party's support. He became the first African American to run for mayor of Trenton.

It was generally believed that the first African American to cast a ballot in a general election was John Smith of the Fifth Ward. This newfound experience was a great moment for the community. Many believed that they would never see the day that an African American would be allowed to cast a vote that would impact on his future. One aged man who voted for the first time walked out into the middle of the street, took off this hat and declared: "Thank God for that—I'm a Man—Hurrah for the Union."

This spirit reflected the community's joy of having finally achieved the goal that many only dreamed of. Such jubilation could only be matched with high expectations for perhaps seeing the day when full equality would be experienced by all people regardless of color.

The African American Republicans were determined to show they were a potential power to be reckoned with:

> Colored voters were marched in procession yesterday along State Street with a captain at their head, as if to overawe those who do not look favorably on their acquisition of the franchise, plainly showing that the party wishing to make capital out of them had not neglected their training. (*Daily True American*, April 12, 1870)

It is to Anthony Fisher's credit that he dared place his name in nomination for mayor. The tremendous backlash struck fear into many Fifth Ward residents who were afraid of retribution if they were to have voted for Fisher. The city police of the Fifth Ward, to insure that the vote remained loyal to the regular Republican Party, began to take a count and record of all Fifth Ward residents. Their names were checked against court records to determine whether any had felony arrest records. Thus, many African American voters feared for their jobs and their freedom. They also needed to fear for their lives as the following account shows:

John Ricord, the colored man who was quite elated at the idea of casting his first vote came down to the First Ward polls with the astounding intelligence that three men had been killed in the Fifth Ward. Upon being interrogated as the manner of their "taking off" putting his hands on the ballot, he said "Dis feller killed 'em," and walked off in a laugh, the dimensions and volubility of which astonished all the bystanders. (*Daily State Gazette*, April 12, 1870)

Due to tremendous pressure from Republicans, the Fifth Ward rejected overwhelmingly the Fisher candidacy. Fisher received only four votes for mayor out of a total of 695 cast, sixty-five of which were African American voters. Consequently, the Republicans easily outdistanced their Democratic opponents to recapture city government with the help of the African American community which faithfully voted the straight party ticket. (*Daily True American*, April 12, 1870)

The result of the Spring elections in this state proves two things conclusively.

First, that the colored voters are all Republicans, and are certain to support that party in the future.

Second, that New Jersey will go overwhelmingly Republican next fall.

The colored voters being an untried and unknown element in the politics of this state, very naturally the Republicans felt some anxiety as to the test, while the Democrats oscillated between the depth of despair and some faint glimmerings of hope. Animated by the fact of their traditional success in manipulating the foreign element, the

Democrats expected to be able to at least control a considerable portion of the colored vote by the same tactics, and so, brought all their resources of cunning and strategy to bear upon it. The result has triumphantly vindicated the intelligence, sagacity and faithfulness of the colored voters. For ourselves, we never doubted them. We remembered, with too vivid emotions of gratitude, the devoted faithfulness of the colored men to the Union cause all through the war, to permit us to doubt their fidelity to the party which has rescued them from bondage and placed them upon a political equality with the whites. The Democrats have always made the grave mistake of underrating the intelligence of the colored people. (*Daily State Gazette*, April 14, 1870)

The historical significance of the Fisher candidacy is that it did serve warning upon the Republican Party that should it fail to serve as a representative voice for African Americans of Trenton, they would be only too happy to represent themselves. They had taken note from Frederick Douglass. Douglass, the internationally renowned abolitionist, in a debate with William L. Garrison, a white abolitionist who wanted to be remembered for having freed the slaves, stated, "Liberation is only as good as your ability to liberate yourself. No one can do it for you."

Many whites, meanwhile, felt that the Republicans had abandoned traditional values. Consequently, many white Republicans began to leave the party. The number one reason for crossover was said to be "military despotism and negro supremacy policy of Congress." Thus, the city of Trenton was in its embryonic stage as a Democratic city. Much was made of the fact that Robert Lincoln, son of the late President, was considering a run for Congress in Illinois as a Democrat.

Voter Convention of 1872

That the Republicans of the city had begun to take the African American community for granted was an understatement. Meanwhile, the Democrats either ignored the African American vote, paid for African American election favors, or merely sought to incite the white community to fear African Americans and retaliate by voting the Democratic line.

A statewide African American voter convention was called in April 1872 in the city. About fifty delegates met at Temperance Hall. Rev. J. I. H. Swares of Newark filled the post of president, Rev. John D. Blackwell of secretary. Both men served in a temporary capacity with Nathaniel Durham later being chosen as permanent president and Blackwell remaining secretary.

Each delegate paid $1.00 to defray the cost of the convention. Members of the convention endorsed presidential candidate General Ulysses S. Grant for his military as well as political careers, as well as the administration of the affairs of government. Charles Sumner, senator from Massachusetts, was lauded for his supplement to the Civil Rights Bill, while others including Schurz and Trumbull were condemned. All state, local and national officials who blocked the rights of African Americans were deemed "unworthy of their positions and unfit to administer the law and ought to be removed." The fact that African American men were not placed on juries was declared an obnoxious act. The sheriff of Mercer County and the U.S. marshall who witnessed these acts were called upon to resign. School segregation was lambasted. The press was condemned for one-sided journalism. It was felt that the African American population was merely seeking the same rights which other men already enjoyed. Members of the convention declared that they would no longer be puppets.

The net effort of the Voter Convention of 1872 served as a sounding board for social and political problems. The results were minimal and the overall conditions of the African American community were left unchanged, for there was no adoption of resolutions about jury duty representation, the normal school or the anti-black schools of Hoboken. But there was unanimous approval of a resolution endorsing the reelection of President Grant. (Bill Dwyer, *Bygone Days*, *Sunday Times Advertiser*, April 9, 1972)

It was at this time that several African American political organizations were formed. One such organization was the Union Republican Club, led by Captain Harrison. The club had its own drum corps and its members wore tan-colored high hats and carried canes. They met at 31 Bellevue Avenue. Membership included Harry C. Baker, president; William Carey, secretary; and Algernon Frost, treasurer.

The Union Republican Club took part in many political affairs including parades, picnics and rallies. There were many other social and political organizations: the Lincoln Pioneer Corp, the Lincoln Guards, the Veteran Soldiers' Republican Association, the

Garfield Republican Club, the Excelsior Cornet Band (always seemed to be on hand for a historical political event), the Central Republican Club and the Eclectic Club. These clubs would dress in their regal splendor and participate in weekly torchlight parades that had become quite popular in the 1880s.

Many of the newly organized Republican clubs met in the homes of members or held an appointed spot that was generally accepted as a public meeting hall. The Republican Party, however, held most of its meetings at the Princessville Inn. The Princessville, or Red Tavern Inn, was about five miles outside Trenton in what is presently Lawrence Township. African American as well as white Republicans met at the inn to drink and rally support for local as well as national Republican figures; Princessville Inn was a lively area noted for numerous community activities aside from political affairs.

> The commodious service of the inn more than any-
> thing else was probably the reason why Princess-
> ville itself was the center of considerable activity at
> these times, and it was probably the reason why
> these county conventions were popular there. It was
> natural that the party gatherings brought consider-
> able excitement to the locals, bringing crowds of
> people inside the tavern and out. Scores of gigs and
> wagons lined the roadside; little knots of leaders in
> earnest discussion exchanged opinions with political
> war horses or else swapped familiar stories of their
> trade. At these times there was always the aroma of
> a barbequed pig as well as the inviting atmosphere
> of vegetables being stewed by the open fire. Usually
> after dinner the nominations came, accompanied by

lengthy speeches and cheering. There was always
something of the social gathering at these meetings.

One of the greatest rallies held at the Red Tavern-
Princessville Inn was the Republican Convention in
the fall of 1884:

> During the time when conventions were held here
> the proprietor was William Webster Mershon, a
> member of a family who played prominent roles in
> Trenton and Lawrence Township history. Mine host
> Mershon purchased the place from William Hart. It
> is said that Hart bought the tavern from James
> Burk, a native of Ireland.

The area surrounding the Inn (on Princeton Road
leading to the Tavern) is a small cemetery where, as
has been previously stated, whites and African Americans are interred.

In the African American community, one of the
most politically influential of the groups was the
Eclectic Club. It was organized on February 2, 1877,
and had its headquarters for many years at 6 North
Broad Street, next to the old City Hall, northeast
corner of Broad and State Streets. Leaders included
Robert Henri Herbert, John M. Herbert, William J.
Conover and others. Conover was treasurer of the
organization for over thirty years.

Although originally organized as a social club that
catered to "elite" African Americans, the club addressed many political issues, often protesting social
and racial injustices. At one point, for instance, the
Eclectic Club played a role in trying to restore James

The Princessville Inn, home of many an African American Republican rally

W. Crippen to his job as a janitor in the office of the state treasurer. The club noted that Crippen was "the only colored man of either influence or respectability at present employed by the state of New Jersey. To remove him without cause from his present position (humble as it is) would, in reality, deprive the colored people of their only representative in the state service."

A major milestone in the history of the Eclectic Club was its tenth anniversary celebration, at which the featured speaker was Frederick Douglass. At the same occasion, the club received a letter from former President Grant thanking the group for extending an honorary club membership to him. Others who sent messages were President Grover Cleveland, Mrs. John R. Lynch, wife of the ex-congressman from Mississippi, P. B. S. Pinchback, ex-governor of Louisiana, and others. The club had such vast appeal that it survived until 1915.

R. Henri Herbert: The *Sentinel* Man

If the Eclectic Club was one of the foremost organizational voices in the African American community, its longtime president Robert Henri Herbert, known as Henri, was one of its most prominent and outspoken individuals. Perhaps no one person did more to guide the political and social affairs of the community than Herbert. Born in 1857 to Mansfield and Ellen Herbert, R. Henri became a leading figure in the Republican Party, not only at the local but also at the state and national levels.

Early Life of Herbert

Herbert was raised in South Trenton at 25 Lamberton Street. His parents came from Maryland to Trenton where Mansfield opened up a picture frame and showcase manufacturing business during the Civil War. The Herbert family was a large, self-educated, proud family, who made up the middle class or "colored elite." Henri's sisters and brothers were John, Ida, Susan, Gustaves, and Tillie. Henri was educated in the German Catholic and public schools in Trenton. In 1874, while only seventeen years of age, Henri served as a reporter for the *Plainfield State Republican*, and in 1875 he was promoted to business manager. By 1878, he had returned to Trenton where he was employed as a teacher in the Ringold Street School for Colored Children. He also served in various newspaper positions for the *Daily State Sentinel, Daily Free Press*, and in 1880 he founded the *Sentinel*, the first African American weekly in Trenton, which ran until 1883 when it merged with the *Trenton Herald*. In 1884 Herbert became secretary to ex-Senator Blanche K. Bruce who was at that time Registrar of the United States Treasury. Later he served as honorary commissioner from New Jersey in the Department of Colored Affairs. In 1886 Herbert became associated with Martin Lehmann in the manufacturing of cigars at 214 South Broad Street.

A staunch Republican, Herbert held several positions within the Republican Party. In 1881 he was appointed doorkeeper for the New Jersey State Senate (1881-83).

R. Henri Herbert
President of the Eclectic Club

Herbert Family's Home
on Lamberton street, South Trenton

Old Lincoln School

Herbert was a dapper dresser who was always seen with a hat and cane. He was articulate and quite well-read in addition to being a world traveler. He came from a very large family whose political and social roots predate the Civil War, and remained a confirmed bachelor living his entire life in the very home in which he was born.

Herbert was a remarkable person who was as skilled a politician as he was a newspaper editor. The *Sentinel* at one point could boast of having the second largest circulation in the city. (*Sentinel*, October 7, 1882)

It was through the *Sentinel* that Herbert was able to marshall support for many of the political issues that confronted the African American community of Trenton. Because he was a staunch Republican, Herbert found it difficult to support any major challenge to the regular Republican organization; however, he did challenge the Republican structure from within as chairman of the Central Republican Committee. In 1880 when several leading Republicans across the state organized a Colored Convention in Trenton, Herbert unleashed the full weight of his editorial arsenal against the convention.

From 1880 until 1883, Herbert pricked the conscience of the Trenton community, both black and white, to move in a forward and progressive direction. Because Herbert had the only forum by which African American views might be aired fully, he became the community spokesman. His editorial could either make or break a political issue.

It would appear that the only time Herbert broke with the Republican Party was when the Democrats

R. Henri Herbert Ball Team

The R. Henri Herbert Baseball Team of years ago. Reading from left to right: Bottom row—William Lamont, John Feasters, George W. Pugh, George Wright. Top row—Niel Davis, James Lamont, Leon McDaniels, Albert Buckman, Joseph O'Neill. Walter Caminade was the manager. This photograph was taken around the turn of the century. It is by courtesy of George W. Pugh.

put forth a candidate that tended to be better on race relations than the Republican candidate, for although Herbert was a staunch supporter of the Republican Party, he appeared to be an even greater supporter of his own people.

In one editorial, he chastised the Republican Party's lack of respect for African Americans:

> There is no disguising the fact that the black Republicans who have been honest, faithful and influential in their support of the party, have been treated shabbily, meanly, unjustly. They have had the treachery and corruptibility of the dusky rabble forever thrown in their faces; they have been held accountable for every ignorant, worthless negro who sold his vote on election day; no matter how intelligent, high characterized and worthy they may be; they have been uniformly treated upon the principle that "all negroes are alike"; and whenever some slight crumb of recognition has been awarded to the party's "black allies," it has generally been thrown to some fossilized old "uncle" who knew little and amounted to less.
>
> There is no doubt about it, such "management" of the colored vote must necessarily prove abortive. The colored voter of today is not the same individual that he was ten years ago.... Few of this second generation know aught of slavery, save as a historical fact which will ever remain a damning blot upon the record of the American Republic....
>
> Clearly then the days of the hat-under-his-arm-please-give-us-culled-people-som ethin'-boss kind of leader of the colored people are ended. The leadership of "uncle," whose chief recommendation is that he was a good servant, and of the Hon. Mr. so-and-

so's man, who argues that the colored people
should vote for the Republican candidate for town
constable because Abraham Lincoln freed the slaves,
don't amount to much nowadays. And yet these are
the very kind of ignoramuses who possess the
confidence of and receive favors at the hands of
white Republicans as the "representatives" of the
colored race....

The natural place of the black voter is in the
ranks of the Republican Party. All other things
being equal, ninety out of every hundred honest
ones among them would rather remain there than
seek new party affiliations. The platform of the
party and its record of public measures during the
past twenty years are all right. Treat him half way
fairly and the black voter, wherever he is worth
having, will be and remain a Republican.

And now, how is that to be done?

By treating him the same as the balance of the
party are treated. Some black men sell their votes.
That is bad and it is wicked to buy them; but, if
you do, consider that so far as that individual
dusky rascal is concerned, that forfeits all claim he
may ever have had upon the party—but don't hold
the race responsible for him. Some honest black
men are very ignorant, and yet they want office;
commiserate their misfortune, but let them wait
until they learn something before they get the office.
Give the young men, who know something and
amount to something, a chance.... (*Sentinel*, September 16, 1882)

Herbert was considered one of his era's most
eloquent leaders. He accepted numerous positions
within the state. He died on October 12, 1909, at the

age of 52, in the middle of the street on Princeton
Avenue near Trent Street. The headline of the day
read: "R. Henri Herbert Found Dead in the Street Last
Night." (*Trenton Times*) There is some mystery surrounding his death. It is believed that he died of heart
failure, while other accounts stated that he died of
apoplexy. He was discovered by two motormen who
revealed that he was found with his hat and coat
nearby.

The death of the *Sentinel* man left a void in the
African American community, for Herbert had been
recognized as an unchallenged leader. He had presid-
ed over an important period in the political development of African American Trenton.

Civil Right Legislation

During Herbert's time, African American leadership
rallied support for the Republican ticket. The Republicans responded with several pieces of progressive
legislation including the desegregation act of 1881 (at
the state level) and the national Civil Rights Act of
1875. This act outlawed discrimination on the basis of
race in public places. The first active challenge to the
act was recorded in the Trenton Billiard Parlor Case.
Horace Deyo and Henry Onque were two African
American men who were refused permission to play
billiards in the Trenton House saloon on March 15,
1875. Both men brought suit under the new civil rights
act. The decision was rendered by E. Mercer Shreene,
U.S. Commissioner, in the case of the United States vs.
Peter Katzenbach. Deyo and Onque lost when Shreene

ruled that "the billiard parlor was a private business of a private party conducted as suits the keeper. It is no more a place of public amusement than a drinking saloon, the applicant may be refused and driven away for reasons best known to the owner and which he is not bound to disclose. The Civil Rights Bill has nothing to do with and was not intended to have anything to do with such places." (*Weekly Public Opinion*, April 1, 1875)

Statewide civil rights protections were instituted with the passage of the 1884 New Jersey Civil Rights Act.

Republican Ups and Downs

The Republicans were also instrumental in engineering patronage positions for loyal supporters. The positions included public jobs in municipal or state office buildings or in schools. They were eagerly sought after with much political horse trading; if one wanted to be a waiter, janitor or window cleaner in a municipal or state building, the appointment had to be cleared by the Republican leadership which had to be thoroughly convinced of steadfast support for the party. The job of doorkeeper in the state legislature was one of the major prizes in the African American patronage roll. Herbert served as doorkeeper from 1881-1883. Such positions carried much prestige within the community, especially since no African American held any elected position.

The African American community supported the Republican Party from 1870 up to 1932. The *Sentinel* boasted of "twenty-one Afro-American candidates" who were in line for the position of doorkeeper in the New Jersey legislature—and "four wards yet to hear from." Indeed one had to follow the hard line support for the party. The African American Trenton Garfield and Arthur Republican Club expelled some of its members because the leadership felt that the members had committed "Democratic heresy" through their support for certain local Democratic candidates. (*Sentinel*, 1880)

The relationship of the African American community to the Republican Party was by no means an ever smooth experience. There were numerous incidents in which the African American community had to direct the attention of the Republicans to their particular needs. One such issue was the following:

WHY IS THIS THUS?

An old-time Republican asks Mr. Chas. H. Skirm a pertinent Question—What is a man who promises one thing and does another?
—An Unenviable Position

To the Editor of the *Sentinel*:

Why is it that the Sheriff of Mercer County has never put any of your race on the panel of jurors for the County Courts? I labored hard to secure Mr. Skirm's election, not simply because I am a Republican, but because I believed that he was a fair, liberal man, who would dare to do what was right.

I expected he would at least do the colored people justice in this matter, for I know that he promised to do so. I see that colored jurors have been drawn for the County Courts in Louisville,

Ky., Huntsville, Ala., Athens, Ga., Galveston, Texas, and in many other places in the South. In Virginia, where the county Sheriffs have neglected to do it, the United States Courts have compelled them to.

This prejudice against a man because he is dark colored has got to die out. But you must not be afraid to demand your rights. It is your duty to redress their wrongs, through *The Sentinel*. You need not fear that you will lose by it. The people like your paper and they are going to take it, even if your reporter is a little enterprising at times.

Mr. Skirm is violating a law by refusing to do the same by your people that he does by others; besides, he places himself in the position of breaking his own word. Look after it. It is your duty.

Yours for justice,

B.
Trenton, N.J.
10, 23, 1880

An additional source of frustration was the fact that the Republican State Committee had been organized without any African American representation despite the efforts of the community to secure membership at the State level:

The effort to secure a colored member of the State Executive Committee was in all respects a commendable one, and although it failed among the delegates from the Third Congressional District, we had hoped that in the appointment of the four members-at-large the Hon. George M. Robeson would have given the 18,000 colored Republican voters one representative. (*Sentinel*, 1880)

Undaunted by the snub of the Republican State Committee, the community formed its own New Jersey Colored Republican State Committee:

MEETING OF THE NEW JERSEY COLORED REPUBLICAN STATE COMMITTEe—A meeting of the N.J. Colored Republican State Committee was held at the Eclectic Club rooms, in this city, on Wednesday. Capt. E. J. Jordan, of Hudson, in the Chair, and Jesse Lawson, of Plainfield, acted as Secretary. A permanent organization was effected, and Mr. Chas. N. Robinson, of Camden, was chosen as Chairman, and Jesse Lawson, of Union, Secretary. Rev. J. H. Bean, of Burlington, was made Vice President, and J. W. Mays, of Camden, Treasurer. The following named gentlemen were appointed a Committee on Finance: David D. Turner, Salem; W. S. Gorden, Mercer; W. F. Powell, Burlington; G. B. Hall, Union; and J. W. Mays, of Camden. The following resolution offered by Mr. W. F. Powell was adopted:

Mr. W. F. Powell offered a resolution that the chairman of the committee fill all vacancies, and that the cities of Trenton, Camden and Newark be entitled to separate representation. Adopted.

Mr. W. S. Gordon offered a resolution recommending a State celebration of the twentieth anniversary of the Emancipation Proclamation on the first day of January, 1883. Adopted. (*Sentinel*, 1880)

Despite the problems encountered with the Republicans, African American Democrats were scarce as hen's teeth; indeed, it was considered sacrilegious for an African American man to vote for a Democrat. Consequently, the Mercer County Democratic Party did not attempt to recruit African American members. Recognizing that the "colored vote" had become a formidable opposition in the city, the Democrats resorted to buying African American votes. The sale of votes to the Democrats prompted this editorial response from the *Sentinel*:

TO THE COLORED PEOPLE

You are an important factor in Mercer county politics. Your vote is the balance of power. Use it properly and you can make it the means of your social, educational, and moral elevation; and a great and almost irresistible leverage towards securing you avenues through which to amass wealth and obtain power.

You need these things. You haven't got them. You can get them with your vote. Destiny has decreed that you must endeavor to get them through the Republican Party.

But you can't do it if you sell your vote. Use it with judgment. Use it in wisdom.

And this year it is the highest wisdom to cast it for the Republican candidates.

The appeal appeared to have some effect, for on Election Day the Democrats were soundly rejected by African American voters.

Perhaps because the Republicans had taken the African American vote for granted, or perhaps because the community wanted to exercise some political independence, or both, a statewide African American convention was organized in Trenton, much to the chagrin of local and state Republican officials. The convention, set for July 1880, did not receive the backing of the *Sentinel*. In fact, the *Sentinel* did everything possible to discourage Trenton residents from participating. The editor predicted that the convention would be a failure. The paper ran numerous editorials denouncing the convention as being divisive and outside the mainstream of the regular Republican Party structure.

Henry Highland Garnet Visits Trenton

It was at this time that one of the leading African Americans in the country visited Trenton. That person was Henry Highland Garnet, a leading advocate for civil rights. Second only to Frederick Douglass, Garnet commanded tremendous respect in the African American communities across the nation. Upon his arrival in Trenton, there was considerable speculation that he might attend the convention and address the delegates. The *Sentinel* was quite unrelenting in its attack on the convention. Garnet, who stayed in Trenton the entire week of the convention, did not attend any of its sessions. He did, however, send a message of address to the delegates by way of the *Sentinel*:

CHANGE THE TIME

Dr. Garnet opposed to the Colored Convention, and advises the Managers to abandon it.

To the New Jersey Convention of Colored Citizens called to assemble in Trenton on the 15th of July, 1880

On my own account, without the request or suggestion of any person or persons, I take the liberty of addressing a few words to the patriotic gentlemen who have united in calling a Convention at the above named place and date. In looking over the columns of *The Sentinel*, I find that many of the leading and influential colored men of this State are of the opinion that the 15th of July is not the proper time for the holding the proposed Convention, as the time named is very unfavorable to the attendance of a large majority of the thoughtful, prudent and sagacious men whose counsel would be valuable to the deliberations of the callers of the meeting. As an older worker in all the grand movements in the cause of freedom and human rights for the last forty-five years, including the work of the abolition of slavery, free soil, liberty party, and the organization and triumph of the Republican Party, may I respectfully suggest that you put off the meeting until the early part of October, and that you in the mean time seek and secure the cooperation of the true and strong men throughout the entire State. There is a great necessity for our colored citizens of this and other States to assemble and make known our grievances and assert our rights before both political parties, and the friends of justice and equality before the Constitution and the laws. Yes, there is need, pressing need for periodical and frequent counsel among our people, as no one can deny that in the South our boasted rights are but "as sounding brass and a tinkling cymbal," and in the North we are valued but for little more than our votes. "Agitate, and agitate, and agitate," as Daniel O'Connell used to say, until in every part of our broad land, a man shall be regard-

ed as a man without respect to race, color or previous condition of servitude. Brethren, change the
time of the Convention.

Signed,

HENRY HIGHLAND GARNET
Trenton, July 10th, 1880

Mr. J. P. Johnson Howard, who addressed the Colored
Convention, was the:

first colored man in the U.S. Diplomatic Service,
and was a Sherman delegate to the Chicago Convention. He is a New York lawyer who enjoys a
lucrative practice. Speaking of the Convention, he
said, "I am of the opinion that it is a poor thing; we
can accomplish nothing by it; I am opposed to it
and regret that it was called, although I am, as a
rule, in favor of separate colored organizations
where any good can by accomplished by them."

In another report, the *Sentinel* noted,

Mr. W. F. Powell, of Burlington, one of the Secre-
taries, said: "I think the time was unfortunate.
Again, we don't want any Colored Convention;
these separate bodies tend to keep up the spirit of
caste. We should demand our rights as Republicans,
not as a separate class." (July, 1880)

All these accounts plus several others were carried in
the *Sentinel*. R. Henri Herbert had used the power of
the press to halt Trenton's support for the convention.
The *Sentinel* published several editorials regarding the

Colored Convention and not one was favorable. In this sense, it appeared that the *Sentinel* had taken on the role of supreme guardianship of African American concerns. Largely through the undaunted efforts of editorial and journalistic sabotage orchestrated by the *Sentinel*, and to some degree the failure of Henry Highland Garnet to attend, the convention was a dismal experience. Herbert could boast later that Trenton did not support the convention: "Not a single Trenton man sat in the Colored Convention on Thursday as a delegate."

Politics of Change Leaves African Americans on the Outside Looking In

The late 1880s to the early 1890s saw a shift in political philosophy of the Republican Party at the national level. Ohioan Rutherford B. Hayes had entered into an unholy alliance with Southern Democrats in order to become President. At the national level the Republicans seemed more interested in "tariff reform and free trade." It appeared now that the party of Lincoln and emancipation had moved away from social legislation and had become more concerned with conservative matters.

At the national level, African Americans who had entered Congress were being ousted by the Republican leadership in their states.

Locally, the Republican Party had begun to show signs of change. African Americans felt that they no longer had a stake in the regular Republican organization. Consequently, several organizations were formed to underscore the need for a new direction including the Colored Men's Independent Political Club (1888-89), whose members included John Seruby, president; William Somers, secretary; and Charles Schench, treasurer. They also began to organize their own state committee. This committee was organized with the blessings of R. Henri Herbert who had fought such a move as being divisive fifteen years earlier. It met in the rooms of the Eclectic Club, a club virtually owned and controlled by Herbert. The Colored Republican State Committee which met on North Broad Street was led by Colonel W. W. Murrell of Monmouth County as its president. Zach De Kline of Jersey City was elected vice president and Dr. G. W. Rutherford of Newark was made chairman of the executive committee.

The club departed from the national Republican Party line with the adoption of several resolutions, including calls for nonintervention in South America:

> Resolutions of sympathy for the Cuban patriots, and others advising that undo haste be avoided in acting on the Venezuelan question were adopted.
>
> A legislative committee of nine members was appointed to urge such legislation as it deems best for the colored people of the state. This committee will ask Governor Griggs to retain in his employ, as messenger, Samuel Gordon, who has faithfully served so many governors. (*Daily True American*, January 23, 1896)

This break alarmed the Republican Party, which feared losing a loyal bloc of votes that appeared to be drifting in a different direction.

The African American community of Trenton had become a bit sophisticated in its approach to community politics. While still loyal supporters of the Republican Party, there was some distinction being made with regard to its local and national philosophy. The organizational structure tolerated this unwarranted as well as unwanted break within the Republican ranks; however, with national as well as local attention being focused on somewhat different issues, the African American community was in political limbo. There was no place to go. The Democrats were openly hostile to social reform and the Republicans were clearly ambivalent. It was as if uninvited guests had come for dinner and no one present possessed the strength of character to ask the intruders to leave. Thus, the African American Republicans remained for the meal but were forced to eat in servants' quarters from paper plates while the invited guests dined in splendid opulence, with neither side fully taking responsibility for the inevitable need to come to terms with the situation.

The Saga of Poke Hutchins

The turn-of-the-century rise and decline of Theodore (Poke) Hutchins in many ways symbolized the shift in the African American community's alliance with the Republican Party. Like Henri Herbert, a member of the Eclectic Club, the colorful Hutchins was a central figure in the political arena. If Herbert was the primary spokesperson for the community, Hutchins was the key man for the nitty-gritty aspects of getting out the vote. So skillful was Hutchins at managing the African American vote that he was referred to in political circles as "King."

Hutchins ran a saloon and gambling house at 2 Belvidere Street in Trenton where the Republican leaders would gather, drink and plot political strategy. The saloon was ultimately designated as Republican Party headquarters for the Thirteenth Ward. Hutchins provided plenty of entertainment and the ward became known as the "Red Light District." Vice and violence were part and parcel of the raucous scene at Hutchins' saloon. Even Hutchins himself was the victim of assault in his own establishment, as the *Daily True American* reported:

> Theodore Hutchins, alias "Poke," the colored Republican leader, got a little rough handling last night at the hands of his constituent, Hugh Collins of 38 Fowler Street. Collins is now at the Central Police Station and "Poke" will appear against him this morning to prefer a charge of assault and battery.
>
> Collins got into a fight with his wife at their home and she ran to "Poke's" saloon to telephone to the police. Collins, after learning that "Poke" allowed her to use the phone, went to "Poke's" place and, it is said, left the imprint of his fist on "Poke's" face.
>
> "Poke" himself then brought the telephone into play and asked police headquarters for assistance.

Patrolman Murphy was sent to "Poke's" rescue and bundled Collins off in the patrol wagon, leaving "Poke" in the bar room nursing his badly wounded pride. (*Daily True American*, 1902)

Hutchins permitted these conditions because it was good for his business. His hold on the African American vote was strong, and he was considered a member of the "elite." Hutchins was a keen political animal who knew how to manipulate his influence. If a person was arrested in his saloon, Hutchins would often provide the money for bail and go to court with the defendant. While in court, he would counsel the judge on the circumstances surrounding the incident and often determine the outcome of the verdict. By supporting his patrons, he insured that they returned to his business for more fun and that they supported Hutchins politically.

Hutchins' crafty political behavior became his own undoing. Since the saloon was constantly the scene of trouble, the "King" began to receive bad press. One controversy involved Hutchins' defiance of a taboo against allowing white women to patronize an African American drinking establishment. He even went so far as to allow two white women to marry colored men in his place of business. After considerable political pressure, however, Hutchins moved to deny white women access to the saloon. "These women ... are now without a place to spend their evenings," the newspaper reported, "because Poke has ruled that colored politics and white women do not go well together." It was also at this time that he was indicted for running a disorderly house.

Undaunted by the controversy, Hutchins announced his own candidacy for council in the Thirteenth Ward. This move caused alarm among whites who lived in the Thirteenth Ward and did not want Hutchins to represent them. It was an even greater cause for concern among Republican leaders who never dreamed that one of their key ward leaders would seek to run as a candidate himself. Because of these concerns, Hutchins' influence as a political leader continued the downward spiral begun during the debate over women in his saloon. This decline in standing was readily apparent to many people in the know, with one exception: Theodore "King Poke" Hutchins. As indictments swirled around him, social decay plagued his constituent base and political defection was all too apparent, Hutchins took to higher ground and began to clothe himself in politician's garb, leading what the press called "a rather virtuous life" and attending many church suppers and graveside ceremonies. These tactics were of little use. His political allies all but gone, the House of Cards upon which Hutchins built his political power came crashing down. A case was mounted against him on the basis of charges that robberies were taking place in the saloon:

> Striking evidence of robbing have been committed in the Republican headquarters of the Thirteenth ward, characterized the trial of its proprietor, Poke Hutchins, which was begun yesterday afternoon in Mercer court, on an indictment found by the grand jury, charging him with keeping a disorderly house.

John C. Horn and Benjamin Bayard were the victims and testified that they had been relieved of amounts of more than $20 each while carousing in Poke's drinking rooms.

In each instance, it was inferred that the victims were given "knock-out drops," for they failed to remember anything that transpired shortly after entering the saloon until waking up several hours afterward with money gone and in another place.

The indictment and trial did not seem to affect Hutchins, who believed that his political influence and savvy would in the end prevail and that he would emerge victorious. But a string of evidence was presented against him.

It was clear that Poke was singled out for special treatment for at the same time that he was indicted, an Italian ward leader for the Republican Party named Tony Marolda was indicted for the exact same crime and was even likened to "Poke."

The two trials were argued at virtually the same time. Their circumstances were nearly identical. Both men were ward leaders, both garnered votes for the Republican Party in their respective communities, both ran saloons and both were indicted for running a disorderly house; both appealed to the Republican leadership for aid and both were rejected. Yet the outcome of the trials was quite different. Marolda received two months in prison, while Hutchins was given a year.

It can be seen that Poke's trouble began in earnest when he decided to run for political office. Prior to his announcement as a candidate, he enjoyed wide support in the African American community. He became a threat, however, when he tired of being the follower and endeavored to be the leader:

> The fear for the party's success in next fall's election, which has taken hold of the Republican leaders of the Thirteenth Ward since "Poke" Hutchins announced himself a candidate for common council a couple of weeks ago while under arrest at the Central Police Station, has caused them to put forth extra efforts to dump the colored leader.
>
> In order to regain some of the party's lost reputation and also a little more respectability to its claims for support, the leaders are using R. L. Dobbins, the hatter of East State Street, who resides on Bellevue Avenue, to enter the race against the "king of the red light district."
>
> Mr. Dobbins has not yet expressed the willingness to take up the fight, and the Republicans of the Thirteenth Ward are in rather sore straits to get a candidate to whom they can place enough confidence to regain what "Cy" Barnhard lost last fall.
>
> Whether Street Commissioner John Ginder will figure in the naming of Poke's opponent rests entirely with the voters, who showed their attitude to Ginder's rule by giving his protege the icy hand in the last election.

The politicians abandoned Hutchins purely for political reasons and his indictment was timed to crush his political ambitions.

Politics After Hutchins

With the destruction of the Hutchins machine came a
new awareness for the African American community.
Hutchins was sent to prison, his place was closed and
later reopened by William Higgins. Initially, John H.
Walton had sought the permit but was rejected, for he
lacked political clout. Higgins, on the other hand, was
granted the license for having performed services for
City Hall. Granting Higgins a license was an agoniz-
ing affair for the Republicans, however, because they
did not want to lose the African American vote while
at the same time they did not want to boost Higgins
too much and lose the established black Republican
leaders. It appeared that Higgins was not politically
connected to the African American Republican machine set forth by Hutchins and Herbert. Hutchins'
followers felt that they had been betrayed by the
Republican Party, and they vowed to put up a fight.

Now the Republican Party was in deep political
trouble. Candidates were "flying at each others'
throats" in order to land the nomination. Before
Hutchins was forced from the race, the Republicans
had convinced R. L. Dobbins to enter the race to serve
as a spoiler for Hutchins, who clearly had the edge.
Now with Hutchins gone, as the candidates began to
jockey for position, the African American community
began to shift in a new direction.

The successor to Hutchins was Clarence Reynolds.
Reynolds was a trusted Hutchins associate and he
vowed revenge on the Republican machine. With the
departure of Hutchins came the demise of the red
light district, but not the demise of politics in the

Thirteenth Ward. The entire City Hall crowd that at one time was quite well received in the community fell into disfavor. The fallout of the Hutchins affair was to have a devastating effect, for Reynolds and his supporters were openly courting the Democratic Party.

A group of men which constituted the Township Committee of Princeton issued an appeal to the community which argued that it was the duty of African Americans to "repudiate the Republican Party," commenting,

> We have been the blind followers of incompetent leaders, whose sole object has been for the benefit of self. The best evidence of Democratic sincerity is the remedy that party has offered for the existing evils. May we, like thoughtful men, take advantage of this opportunity. Friends, the virtues of the Republican Party have long since died out in the ashes of the past and there is none among its leaders generous enough or good enough to rekindle the holy flames.

Consequently some African American leaders abandoned the Republican Party and organized the Frank S. Katzenbach, Jr., Colored Democratic Club. They met at 36 Chancery Street in Trenton. Just five years earlier, such an idea would have been considered out of the question.

While some were switching to the Democratic Party, a small segment of the community proposed that the African American vote become independent. The call for an independent position was made by Rev. I. W. Roundtree:

The departure of the better element of the colored voters from the Republican Party and their union in the support of the Democratic candidates is one of the most notable features of the present campaign.

Several colored pastors, who were disguested [*sic*] with the manner in which the old excise board granted licenses, have taken a stand against brewery influences and are agitating the defeat of the Republican excise ticket. While the granting of a renewal of the license of "Poke" Hutchins may have been pleasing to some of his followers, the better element of the colored people, especially those connected with the different religious denominations became disgusted with the place. They claim that this particular saloon did more to reduce the membership of the colored churches than any other influence which could be brought to bear.

The colored people feel that the alleged debt it owed to the Republican Party has been paid and propose in the future to follow the dictates of their own consciences.

The biggest gain of the Democrats among the colored people is in Princeton where a club known as the Princeton Colored Democrat Club has been organized in the interest of Mr. Hoff, the Democratic candidate for county clerk.

The cause of the departure of the Princeton colored voters to affiliate with the Democratic Party was based upon the raid made upon their clubs and threats of indictment by the grand jury if they did not vote the Republican ticket. (*Daily True American*, October 23, 1902)

Republicans Desperate

The gap between the African American community and the Republican Party was growing even wider. Now for the first time in years, the clergy was taking a position in politics, and a full-scale political battle erupted. With their political fortunes somewhat in doubt, the Republicans became very desperate. There was evidence of voter fraud as the Republicans sought to regain lost ground.

They then reverted to an old tactic first practiced by the Democratic Party nearly twenty years earlier. They began to go into African American businesses passing out checks and literally buying the vote. Street Commissioner John Ginder, an active Republican and arch-enemy of Hutchins, found himself canvassing the Thirteenth Ward on behalf of Anthony Skirm, a candidate for council. Money was given to potential voters and liquor was bought. Before the alcohol was dispensed, the potential voter had to swear to vote the Republican Ginder-Skirm ticket.

Unfortunately for the Republicans, many African American ward residents were rallying around Irvin W. Rodgers, the Democratic candidate for mayor.

Not giving up easily, the Republicans began to make bold and sweeping promises, one of which was to name a young African American man, Charles H. Wilson, as the first African American policeman to the force when the next vacancy occurred. This was merely a promise as the first African American would not be appointed until December 3, 1917, in the person of Vincent Harvey.

The efforts to regain the African American votes were an exercise in futility. On Election Day, the African American voters of the Thirteenth Ward soundly rejected the Republican candidates. Some African American Republicans remained; however, their loyalty left a lot to be desired:

> Because of the energy displayed in Councilman James Buchanan in prosecuting the suit against former receiver of Taxxes [sic] C. Harry Baker, he was made the victim yesterday of considerable cutting on the part of the colored voters, from where Baker receives a large part of his support.
>
> For the first time in many years the Republican election workers were unable to control the colored vote, and in the Thirteenth Ward the custodians of the Republican campaign funds were paying as high as $5 a vote, knowing that Mr. Buchanan was being sacrificed for the rest of the ticket. The colored Republican workers in the ward openly distributed Republican tickets bearing Mayor Katzenbach's pasters [sic]. (*Daily True American,* November 4, 1903)

Political debate became livelier than ever:

> At no time within the past 20 years has such enthusiasm been stirred up by a political meeting in the Thirteenth Ward as was evident at the first rally of the Thirteenth Ward Democratic Club at the club's quarters last evening. Fully 500 voters of that old-time Republican stronghold turned out to hear the campaign issues fairly and honestly discussed.

The first part of the evening's program was a torchlight procession through the streets of the ward. The members of the club, headed by the Bayard Post Band, led the procession, which numbered fully 300.

At the close of the parade the marchers returned to the corner of West Hanover and Calhoun Streets, where a platform had been erected, and a number of speakers were waiting to address the meeting. (*Daily True American*, October 31, 1907)

Thus, politics in Trenton at the turn of the century was up for grabs in the African American community. Some African Americans still continued to vote for the Republican Party—some out of loyalty to the past and some out of habit. Nonetheless, politics and the community of Trenton was anything but business as usual.

Part Four

SOCIAL LIFE OF AFRICAN AMERICAN TRENTON 1890-1900

The political debates which characterized the shifting allegiances of Trenton's African American coincided with a period of significant social change in the community. The population was increasing and new organizations and cultural activities were springing up throughout the city. The right to vote was firmly established, schools were more open than before to African American children and a new militancy and awareness was sweeping the African American neighborhoods.

The Swamp

Much of Trenton was organized along strict racial and class lines. Residential patterns were well established and many African Americans lived in neighborhoods established prior to the American Revolution. There was, however, a large African American community that did not conform to tradition. This community was known as the Swamp. It violated all rules regarding social order in Trenton, for here rich mingled freely with poor, African Americans interacted with whites and crime functioned in the midst of social order.

The community can be traced to a period just following the close of the Civil War. It took its name from a piece of heavy artillery used in the Civil War to shell Charleston Harbor. The weapon was a cannon that had been nicknamed Swamp Angel by Union soldiers. It had been used to discharge the first poison gas shell ever fired into a city. According to *The Trenton Story*, the cannon "was purchased with other condemned weapons and sent to the Trenton Iron Works to be melted down." It was identified and a large community effort was organized to save the cannon from destruction.

The Swamp Angel was later mounted on a public drinking fountain at the corner of North Clinton and Perry Streets. This area included such streets as Allen, Feeder, and Humboldt Streets.

People who lived in that section of Trenton were called "Swampers." The section became known as the Swamp. The Swamp community was largely made up of African Americans. This community was the finest example of hard-drinking-hard-gambling and fast living. Life in the Swamp was a miserable existence, with crime being allowed to flourish. The newspapers were filled with stories relating to crime in the Swamp.

It appeared as though the greatest amount of crime centered on Allen Street. Here in the Swamp lived an

The Swamp Angel, the cannon that started a community

African American woman named Mary Butler who managed to be mixed up in nearly all the disturbances in the Swamp. Mary was a well known "Swamper" who was a thief. On one occasion, she entered the home of Joseph Andrews of 245 Allen Street and when he told her to leave, she struck him and tore his clothing. Upon being placed under arrest, Mary proved so unmanageable that a patrol wagon was summoned. Throughout the entire episode, she continued to declare her innocence, fighting the officers all the way to the station house; and upon being removed from the wagon, a fine gold watch, which had been hidden in one of her stockings, dropped to the ground. She was later ordered to pay a fine of twenty-five dollars or spend six months in the workhouse. (*Daily True American*, January 24, 1896)

The Swamp was not only filled with crime and violence, but also with hopelessness and despair. Life in the Swamp became of such interest that several editorials were carried in the leading Trenton papers, describing the community:

> Within a very few weeks there have occurred many cases of assaults, bordering on to murder, in the slum of the city between Perry Street and the Feeder, which is known as the Swamp. A woman has been nearly killed with a flat iron, another dangerously cut with a knife, and several have been badly beaten. Only the other night one of the residents in a drunken rage fired a revolver point blank at another man, with the evident intention of killing him, and when arrested he resisted the officer and threw him into the gutter.

On the streets which run close by the Swamp are many fine residences, some of them costing as high as $10,000, where wealthy and retired merchants live, but it is almost a nightly occurrence for them to be awakened by shrieks of "Murder" from the under man in a brawl or by the screaming of some woman whose husband is beating the life out of her in a drunken frenzy. Yet it is but seldom that any of these offenders are ever properly dealt with by the authorities, who seem to almost overlook their lawlessness because they are only "Swampers."

It is an apparent fact that this section of the city is becoming more boisterous weekly and that the lawlessness will continue to grow unless sharp discipline is ordered there as it was a few years ago.

There are but few people outside of the "social set" of the Swamp who have ever gone through its dirty streets even out of curiosity, and a visit there would set many a philanthropist thinking as to why the place is not cleaned out, the rickety huts torn down and the denizens scattered in other parts of the city.

A trip through the Swamp in daylight brings pity to a tender heart, and at night the revolting scenes bring disgust. The houses are mostly shells, a couple of stories in height, and some of them contain as many as six families, who make up between them the four or six dollars a month rent, which the whole house costs. The "growler" is the Swamp's greatest evil and there is almost a ceaseless run to and fro with foaming pitchers of beer, whenever there is the price of the filling in the house.

There are colored men with white wives living here, and vice versa. There are houses of loose morals where both colors meet at night and at times through the dirty window panes can be distinguished, the features of young men of well-to-do parents seated beside the ebony damsels drinking beer and all hands smoking and holding a mighty orgie. All of these things are overlooked in the Swamp and nothing but a noisy drunken brawl puts an end to the proceedings.

Besides all this there is a gambling establishment run by a colored man, which is in full operation every night in the week, including Sundays. Sometimes large crowds congregate in his rooms which are on the second floor of a cheap dwelling, and it is said that a high limit poker game is often indulged in particularly on Saturday and Sunday nights. There is no secrecy about the place, and any colored man and most white men with money in their clothes can gain admittance....

The number of old people in the Swamp is large, and among them are many quaint characters, including preachers who have no church, and fortune tellers who have few clients except they be the half-grown girls of the neighborhood. There are also prize fighters, who can handle a brick better than their fists, and numerous of the "masher" clan who change their tattered clothes at nightfall, and robed in someone else's last summer suit, start down the street on a heart-crushing mission.

The Swamp is undoubtedly the city's most wretched slum, and presents as fine a field for charity and the attention of philanthropists as can be found, but aside from an occasional visit of a missionary or a local preacher, the poor people who live there seldom receive attention unless it be from the police.

Goosetown

The African American community of Trenton also began to spread through the city into Goosetown and in and around the Coalport (so named due to the large coal trade business in and around the coal yard); but it was the Swamp, more so than any other community, that caused Trentonians to pause and wonder, for there was sadness interlaced with gaiety, crime was accompanied by religious zeal; and hope was followed with despair.

Much like the Swamp, however not as notorious, was Goosetown, in East Trenton. Sometimes referred to as the Lava Beds, this section of Trenton was located beyond the stone bridge and west of Clinton Avenue, north of Perry and south of the feeder canal. This section of Trenton was called Goosetown because it seems that nearly every resident kept chickens, ducks and geese as well as pigs. As time passed, such neighborhoods as Goosetown, the Swamp, Gallows Hill and the Locust Hill sections of Trenton (sections where African American residents lived upon their early arrival to Trenton) have all but vanished. Little historical record of their existence has survived as a testament to their existence.

Cultural Activities

In spite of the suffering endured by residents of the Swamp, Goosetown and other neighborhoods, cultural activity and sports thrived in the late nineteenth century. Music, dance and theater were abundant. This was the period, for instance, of the famous cake walk dance which became popular in the so-called Gay Nineties. African Americans were encouraged to demonstrate their skills in this dance, and then were rewarded with a cake.

This was a time when Temperance Hall and the Taylor Opera House entertained numerous social events, including the Fisk Jubilee Singers, a gospel choir from Fisk University in Tennessee that traveled worldwide to raise funds for their financially troubled school. The Fisk Jubilee Singers came to Trenton to perform at the Masonic Hall in 1890. Since there were no hotels to accommodate them, they were required to seek lodging within the African American community. The first license was granted to open a hotel and saloon for African Americans in the city in 1894 to Gustaves P. Herbert, brother of R. Henri Herbert and a leader in his own right.

The Minstrel Shows Come to Trenton

The minstrel theater enjoyed a major revival during this period. Although this form of entertainment existed as early as 1860, the 1880s seemed to usher in a reawakened thirst for minstrel shows. This was a time period when local advertisements depicted blacks as mindless, inferior subhumans who were docile and fun loving. Newspapers saw nothing wrong with advertising the sale of "niggerhead buttons"—buttons with a harsh, rough finish.

Minstrel shows featured white men in burnt cork faces who mimicked African Americans in hilarious circumstances. They spoke in broken "colored" vernacular that won rave reviews from whites. Often, the shows would portray an African American man who was poorly dressed and highly uneducated who often matched wits with a white man. The African American would be portrayed as a stereotypical "colored" who could not be trusted, for he would be caught lying, cheating and stealing from the upstanding white man who would always uncover the deeds of the wayward thief before the end of the performance. The African American, once discovered, would be taken to jail and moral of the play would quite often be "never trust the untrustworthy colored man."

The stage acts did much to shape the local prejudices of the white community toward African Americans, for the white community internalized much of what it had seen on stage and accepted it as truth. It neglected to realize that white men wore black face makeup and created circumstances for comedic value. Minstrel shows were of immense importance not so much as a source of entertainment but as a medium to reinforce old stereotypes.

To suggest that minstrel shows were the complete enterprise of whites would be historically inaccurate. There were African American minstrel shows that performed in Trenton. Williams and Walker, an African American minstrel team, performed "Dahomey" at the Taylor Opera House.

> Society was out in force last night at the Williams & Walker production of "In Dahomey" at Taylor Opera House.
>
> The gathering which filled the parquet resembled that which generally greets a big metropolitan production, when silks and satins have a monopoly in the lower part of the house.
>
> The novelty of the performance was that Williams & Walker have the only musical comedy impersonated by a colorer [*sic*] troop on the theatrical circuit. (*Daily True American*, October 28, 1902)

The Williams and Walker performance attracted the elite members of the Trenton community who later raved about the performance:

> A large audience greeted Williams & Walker, playing the musical farce "In Dahomey," in Taylor Opera House last evening. It cannot be said that Williams & Walker were the whole show on the stage as Mrs. Lottie Williams as "Mrs. Stringer," a modiste, was the centre of by-comedy which was by far the cleanest and best work of the evening.
>
> During the progress of the first act "Mrs. Stringer" received her customers and friends in a second-story room and through the open window the most natural comedy was seen and enjoyed by the audience. It was a case of little things well done and the dressmaker divided attention evenly with the stars on the floor of the stage.
>
> In all other things, of course, the interest centered in Williams & Walker, that is, the interest of

the balcony and the "gods," but the parquet found
an intense and amusing feature in the balcony and
the "gods." Seldom have the "gods" been laughed
at so much, but then they were so funny.

All the colored aristocracy were there and they
owned the house. Whenever Williams or Walker
opened their mouths to say something the balcony
and the "gods" were immediately enraptured and
testified by their wealth of applause that the state-
ment was true, that never before in the history of
Taylor Opera House had so many tickets been sold
to colored persons for a single performance.

Williams & Walker won the good will and
plaudits of the white folk in the house, Williams
especially, for his work was the finest example of
"black face" art seen in Trenton for many years;
Walker, for his vivacity makes him a perfect foil for
the lugubrious Williams.

The "marvelous Craig" repeated his former tri-
umphs as a contortionist, as supple as ever; there
seemed not a bone in his body which would not
bend.

All minstrel shows caused significant harm, as the
African American community was powerless to do
anything about them.

The line was drawn, however, with a particular
performance that was to be held at the Taylor Opera
House. This performance was called the Clansman by
Thomas Dixon. The Clansman was the original name
given to the film "Birth of a Nation" by D. W. Griffith.
This motion picture glorified the terrorist Ku Klux
Klan and portrayed African American politicians after
the Civil War as lying, cheating and stealing people

who took advantage of the Southerner. The fact that the Clansman would be performed caused great tension in the African American community. Leaders from every quarter of the city banned together to protest the play.

The battle lines were drawn. Funds were raised and leaders within the political community attempted to enlist the support of the Republican Party to stop the performance. Many white politicians who in one measure or another owed their election to the African American community were prevailed upon to use their political influence. The greatest outcry came from the church leaders.

Rev. H. P. Anderson of Mt. Zion AME Church on Perry Street declared: "It seems to me that in this city [with a] Republican government, which we helped to elect, if the representatives of this party cannot help us stop this play from coming to this city, we ought to have a different party in power." Thus the clergy lead the protest movement in the pulpit and in the community:

> At the request of a committee representing negroes in this city, Princeton and Lawrenceville, a resolution denouncing the play, "The Clansman," as inexpedient and injurious to the people of this community, was adopted at the regular meeting of the Trenton Ministerial union yesterday morning. The resolution evoked considerable discussion.
>
> The "Clansman" resolution was presented by the Rev. J. L. Burton, the Rev. H. P. Anderson and the Rev. L. C. Temple, D.D., all of this city; the Rev. J. V. Peyton, D.D., of Princeton, and the Rev. W. G.

B. Coster, of Lawrenceville. (*Daily True American,*
November 6, 1906)

This pressure caused the mayor to come out against
the presentation.

> The protest of the negroes of this section against the
> production of "The Clansman" tomorrow night will,
> in all probability, be heeded, as Mayor Gnichtel last
> night officially notified the opera house manage-
> ment that the play could not be given until a license
> had been secured from the chairman of the council
> committee on shows and exhibitions.
>
> Chairman Rhodes of the committee states that
> no application for a license has been made. The
> committee meets tonight and the opera house man-
> agement will likely. make application, which, of
> course, will be opposed by the delegation of colored
> clergymen and laymen of this city and surrounding
> towns.

The mayor went on record in opposition to the perfor-
mance. It was to no avail, however, because the Taylor
Opera House ignored the concerns of the African
American community, the mayor and other leaders
who were opposed to the play and presented "The
Clansman."

African American Social Organizations

Because the African American community was pro-
scribed from social activity with whites it was forced
to form clubs and organizations within the communi-

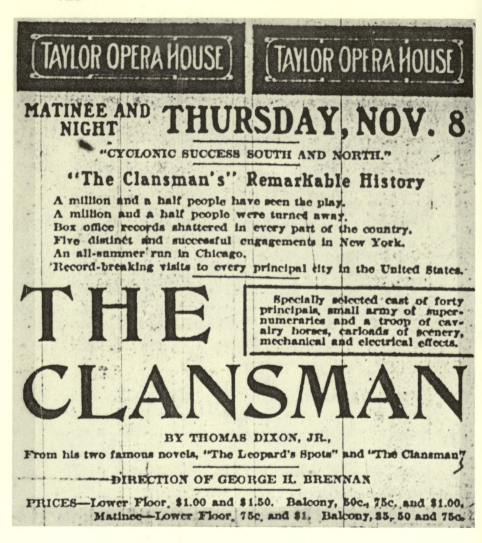

TAYLOR OPERA HOUSE **TAYLOR OPERA HOUSE**

MATINEE AND NIGHT **THURSDAY, NOV. 8**

"CYCLONIC SUCCESS SOUTH AND NORTH."

"The Clansman's" Remarkable History

A million and a half people have seen the play.
A million and a half people were turned away.
Box office records shattered in every part of the country.
Five distinct and successful engagements in New York.
An all-summer run in Chicago.
Record-breaking visits to every principal city in the United States.

THE CLANSMAN

Specially selected cast of forty principals, small army of supernumeraries and a troop of cavalry horses, carloads of scenery, mechanical and electrical effects.

BY THOMAS DIXON, JR.,

From his two famous novels, "The Leopard's Spots" and "The Clansman"

DIRECTION OF GEORGE H. BRENNAN

PRICES—Lower Floor, $1.00 and $1.50. Balcony, 50c., 75c. and $1.00.
Matinee—Lower Floor, 75c. and $1. Balcony, 25, 50 and 75c.

ty. The first social organizations were an outgrowth of the various religious institutions in and about the city. Church socials, picnics, and outings were a very common occurrence in the African American neighborhoods.

There were other organizations that were social in nature yet could not be considered religious. One was the African American Masons, a fraternal order that held much esteem in the community. To be a mason meant social and political acceptance within the African American community and a measure of respect from whites.

The African American Masonic order has had a long and enduring history in Trenton. Consequently, Trenton has never been without a lodge since 1845, when St. John's Lodge was organized. The Masonic body was an integral part of the community. Around 1856, Saint John's Lodge broke with the Grand Lodge and joined the Independents. It was also at this time that Jerusalem Lodge #10 was set up by the National Compact Grand Lodge. Not much is known about Jerusalem other than it lasted until 1865.

> Years ago there was a colored Masonic body in the town bearing the name of King David's Lodge. The headquarters, late in 1871, was on the second floor of St. John's Methodist Church on Woodruff Street, now Allen Street. When that structure took fire late in the afternoon of November 15, 1871, everything belonged to the lodge was destroyed.
> While the history of colored Masons in Trenton is probably lost to record, there is reason to believe that there were some in the town in the 1850s as the

following item from the *Gazette and Republican*, June 25, 1858, would seem to indicate:

> Yesterday was a great day among the colored citizens, there being a grand celebration by the colored order of Free and Accepted Masons. Several lodges arrived from Philadelphia by an extra train, and being joined by their Trenton brethren, they formed a long procession, and preceded by a band of music, and guided by a marshal on horseback, marched through the principal streets and out to Moses' Grove, where the day was spent in listening to speeches, etc. They were in full regalia and presented quite a showy appearance and they seemed to enjoy themselves highly.
>
> In the evening a grand ball at the City Hall wound up the day and the visitors took their departure at a late hour. (Courtesy of Trentonians of the Trenton Public Library, *Trenton in Bygone Days, Some Stage Coach Lines, Sunday Times Advertiser* by Harry J. Podmore)

Saint John and Unity Lodge developed a great rivalry. On December 29, 1875, the same day the two lodges entered into a permanent Masonic Union, the King David Lodge was instituted. At the Grand Session held July 31, 1876, and under Grand Master Charles Nash Robinson, the Lodge was assigned Number 15.

Members met every fourth Thursday at the Shiloh Baptist Church at 104 Belvidere Street. The first officers were: W. John J. Evans, master; Isaac March, senior warden; and Armstead Billups, junior warden. Many lodge brothers who were previously affiliated with Saint John's Lodge merely entered King David Lodge. They included Charles Robinson who would later become the Worshipful Master and Alfred Seruby who served as a representative of Saint John's and worked on the Committee on Account at the Special Communications of January 1878. In some respects one could say that the King David Lodge was an outgrowth of Saint John's, as members of the Saint John's Lodge were essential to the establishment of King David Lodge.

There also was another Masonic order which met in Bordentown, but drew its membership from Trenton. The Masonic Lodge was listed in the Trenton City Directory of 1856: "King Solomon's Lodge, No. 8, of A. Y. M.—Bordentown. William E. Middletown, W. M.; Hudson Wood, S. W.; William Broyden, J. W.; Edward Conover, *Treas.*; Alex. Pardif, *Sec'y*. Meets Monday previous to full moon."

Thus the Masons became a very influential part of the social fabric of the community. On Sunday afternoon, September 30, 1928, the cornerstone of the temple of the Most Worshipful United Grand Lodge Free & Accepted Masons of the State of New Jersey (Prince Hall Affiliation) was laid at 44 Pennington Avenue with impressive ceremonies. The invocation was given by Grand Chaplain T. B. Gibbs and the benediction was offered by Edward Hilton, grand master. Addresses were given by Newton A. K. Bugbee and Mayor Donnelly and E. S. Ballou, grand senior warden. The temple was completed in 1929 and it is now Our Lady of Divine Shepherd Roman Catholic Church.

Another long-lived lodge was the Fort Pillow Lodge No. 3130, Grand United Order of Odd Fellows. By 1892, the lodge held its first grand triennial. The district deputy grand master was R. B. Williams of Princeton. Mr. and Mrs. John H. Jones of Trenton led the grand march.

The Capital Club was a social club founded in the early 1890s. It held its second annual ball on February 20, 1893. (*Trenton Bygone Days*, Journal of Harry J. Podmore) The event included a parade through the streets of the city. Six couples led by R. Henri Herbert, and accompanied by Miss Bessie Worth, took part in the festivities. Others who participated in the activities included: Mr. and Mrs. J. C. Williamson, J. H. Burton and Mrs. Shroeder, Joseph W. Smithy and Miss Olive Bruno, A. Fisher and Mrs. Geneve Howell, J. W. Taylor and Mrs. E. Spencer, J. W. Price and Miss Pekoe, H. Alexander and Miss Marie Joice, and Mr. and Mrs. J. B. Louden. The club held its headquarters at 29 Barnes Street. The following year this site would become the first African American hotel owned and operated by Gustaves Herbert.

There was also the Colored Pioneer Club which was led by Reuben Transom. This social club was very popular during the 1880s and 1890s. It became one of the more popular marching clubs owing to the fact that Reuben Transom was "a strutter." The club later reorganized as a Republican Marching Club and was later referred to as Transom's Guards.

The Excelsior Cornet Band played at such places as the Taylor Opera House and Temperance Hall. The Excelsior Cornet Band trumpeted the gaiety in New Brunswick, New Jersey, when there was a grand statewide celebration of the passage of the Fifteenth Amendment in 1870. The band was probably brought to the celebration by Rev. William E. Walker of Trenton. (*Freedom Not Too Far Distant*, C. Price, p. 140) Yet another important social organization was the Colored Female Temperance Union whose members campaigned against the use of alcohol. The Douglass League, meanwhile, was organized on a nonpartisan basis to celebrate the birthday of Frederick Douglass. The group met in the home of Robert Queen.

African American Union Veterans

There were several organizations that were set up among African American Union veterans who lived in the city. As early as 1856 there was a local military company that was organized under the command of an African American named Budd Pero. (Podmore, *Trentonian*) Consequently it was quite appropriate to organize veterans after the Civil War. One such organization was the Grand Army of the Republic (Colored) (GAR). Chartered on August 18, 1881, it was named Thomas Hamilton Post #56.

The Hamilton Post held its meetings at Bayard Post headquarters. Seventeen members initially signed the roll. They included the following: Commander, Edward Patterson; Senior Vice Commander, Benjamin F. Johnson; Junior Vice Commander, James Sprowell; Adjutant, James B. Crippen; Quartermaster, George S. Johnson; Surgeon, James Brown; Chaplain, John Brown; Officer of the Day, John Dennis; Officer of the

Guard, William Vansyckle; Sergeant Major, Henri
Johnson; and Quartermaster Sergeant, James Riley.

The post lasted into the turn of the century, however, by 1905 only eleven members were left. Others
who attended the encampment were the following:
Samuel Asbury, Commander; Edward Brunno, Benjamin Marsh, Henry Johnson, William VanSickel, Amos
Thompson and John Dennis.

Although not at all a political organization, the
Hamilton Post of the GAR did express its concern
over the termination of an African American janitor.

The Hamilton Post was not the only African American veterans' group. There was also the Sewell Camp
of Colored Civil War Veterans, about which very little
is known, and the Lincoln Pioneer Corps. The latter
was an elite African American social organization
whose members paraded the streets in full uniform
with drum major and band. The corps met at the
corner of Green (now Broad Street) and Hanover
Streets above Anistaki's drugstore. Officers included
A. Crippen, president; J. Byard, secretary and Reuben
Transom, captain. Another such organization was
formed from the Old Garfield and Arthur Campaign
Club. The organization was called Veteran Soldiers
Republican Association. They met in Temperance Hall
and the Washington Market building.

African American Sports

Trenton's African Americans took great pride in their
highly organized and successful participation in the
sporting life. As the century neared its end, sports,

especially baseball, provided an important means for people to come together and work collectively.

The Cuban Giants

Perhaps one of the most, if not the most, respected African American team in Trenton was the Cuban Giants. The Cuban Giants was founded in 1886 by Walter Cook, the financial backer for the team, from Trenton. He placed S. K. Govern, an African American, as manager and made Trenton the team's home base. It is unclear how the name Cuban Giants was generated, other than that African American sports figures, in order to gain recognition and support, were often forced to downplay their North American ancestry:

> When the Babylon club began playing away from home, they passed as foreigners—Cubans, as they finally declared—hoping to conceal the fact that they were just American hotel workers, and talked a gibberish to each other on the field which, they hoped, sounded like Spanish. The New York Giants were even then baseball idols, and so the name, Cuban Giants, was settled upon for the new club. (*Esquire*, 1938)

Pitchers and catchers were paid $18 a week (a handsome sum for the 1880s and 1890s), plus expenses; infielders got $15 and outfielders got $12. The club members included such greats as pitcher Billy Whyte and catcher Clarence Williams. There was also Grant,

Stoney, Fowler and Fleet Walker. The Cuban Giants gained national recognition:

> Their games attracted the attention of the baseball writers all over the country, and the Cuban Giants were heralded everywhere as marvels of the baseball world. They were not looked upon as public freaks, but they were classed as men of talent.... They closed the season of '86 with a grand record made against National League and college teams. (*Only the Baseball Was White*)

Cuban Giants Team Roster, 1886 Season
- Clarence Williams
- Arthur Thomas, catcher
- Billy Whyte
- Shep Trusty
- George Stoney, pitcher
- Jack Frye, first baseman
- George Williams, second baseman
- Abe Harrison, short stop
- Ben Holmes, third baseman
- Bill White, left field
- Ben Boyd, center field

The Cuban Giants took on all comers, including minor league clubs and teams from colleges and universities, as well as semi-pro clubs. Yale, Amherst, Princeton and Penn appeared on the schedule during the late 1880s.

The Cuban Giants by 1887 had attracted such national attention that they were scheduled to play an exhibition game against the champions of the American Association, the St. Louis Browns. Some 7,000 fans

Original Cuban Giants — 1886–1900. St. Augustine, Fla. — Trenton, N.J.

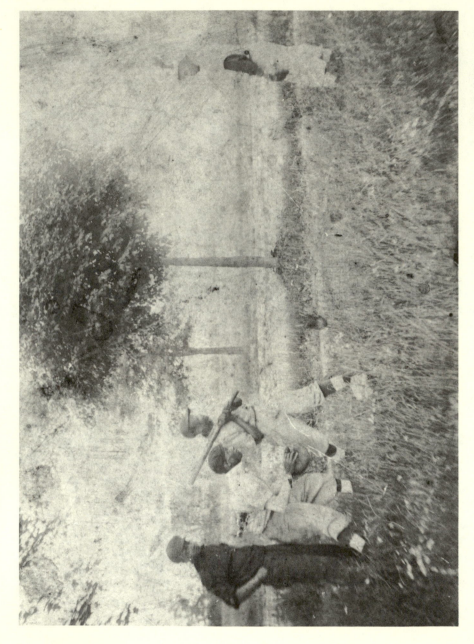

were expected, but the game was never played. The Giants got a telegram stating that the Browns had a great deal of injuries and would be unable to play the exhibition game. The real reason, however, was expressed in a letter written and signed by players of the Brown's club:

> We, the undersigned members of the St. Louis Base Ball Club, do not agree to play against negroes tomorrow. We will cheerfully play against white people at any time, and think, by refusing to play, we are only doing what is right, taking everything into consideration and the shape the team is in at present. (*Only the Ball Was White*)

Of the eight players who signed, four were Northern and a fifth was Canadian.

The Cuban Giants' Popularity Spurred Creation of Similar Teams

The Cuban Giants became so popular that they were no longer looked upon with disfavor by the white community. In fact whites mention the Cuban Giants with a great deal of pride. Trenton promotional material read, "the Cuban Giants, a club of colored professional players, belongs to the Middle States League, and upholds the honor of the city (Trenton) fairly well." (Industries and Advantages of the City of Trenton, 1889, Trenton Board of Trade)

In fact, the Cuban Giants, who experienced no trouble scheduling 150 games—most against white teams—became so popular that numerous teams were formed in hopes of confusing fans. To this end there came into being the Cuban X Giants, the Columbia Giants, Cuban Stars, and so forth. The confusion became so great that the original Cuban Giants brought suit against the Cuban X Giants, but the X Giants replied: "We are informed legally that the name of the Cuban X Giants is not incorporated, and that we have a perfect right to use it."

The Cuban Giants changed their name to the Genuine Cuban Giants. The team name change followed a legal battle to become the sole owner of the name. They also played under the name of the Trenton Club. (*Trenton Times*, 1886)

That the Cuban Giants were popular players seemed to be an understatement. The Cuban Giants attracted thousands to their home field, the Chambersburg grounds. In 1886, for instance, the Giants appeared to be an invincible team that rolled up victory after victory. However, on May 29, 1886, the Giants lost their first game to the St. Louis Champions 9-3. (Dwyer, *Bygone Days*) The crowd in attendance was reported to be 2,000 spectators. On a typical trip, no fewer than seventy-eight men and boys squeezed into a car designed to accommodate less than half that number. Predictably, "the car got stuck" on the Broad Street hill "and all hands had to get out and push her ahead."

On the following day, Decoration Day, the spectators were out again in full force this time for a doubleheader with the Domestics of Newark. The visitors won the morning game 14-5. In the afternoon the Trenton team came through, 18-5.

For weeks thereafter, the Giants, now usually known as the Trentons, continued to attract appreciative crowds, and to defeat such teams as Manayunk, Flushing, the Elites, and the Harrowgates. Signs of trouble began to appear on August 6. The Giants played the Athletics (possibly a forerunner to the Philadelphia A's) 12-1; however, hardly anybody came to the game. "Although yesterday was a pleasant day," the *Times* man wrote, "and a good team was presented, only a small audience was present. It is strange that Trenton cannot support a ball club.... Our people ought to give them patronage."

Later in the season the Trentons played the Gormans who were billed as the Colored Champions of New York. A small crowd was in attendance. After the game the *Times* reporter wrote the following: "Well ... if the coons who attempted to play ball on the Chambersburg grounds yesterday are the colored champions of the great Empire State, heaven help the others they've left behind. Trenton, however, has the honor of having the championship colored team of the United States...." Final score: Trenton 25, Gormans 4.

In the final game of the 1886 season, perhaps its most memorable, the Cuban Giants played the Jersey Blues in Weehawken. Not only did the Cuban Giants win the game, but were honored by a local dignitary in gratitude for their sportsman like conduct on the field.

The Cuban Giants, while by far the most successful, were not the only African American ball club in Trenton. Other clubs included the Trenton Browns, organized by William E. Simpson of Trenton who represented a stock company. Simpson leased the baseball grounds in Chambersburg for the 1886 season. He entered the Eastern League with games set for Washington, Philadelphia, Pottsville, Newark and Princeton. The Browns won their first victory against Princeton, defeating the Princeton club 9 to 5.

There was also the Polka Dot Baseball Club which was formed April 21, 1881. Its members included D. Henderson, Captain; H. Whicoff, President; W. Johnson, Treasurer; and A. Byard, Secretary. They met at 35 West Hanover Street. In their first game the Polka Dot Club defeated the American House nine 16-12.

One team that attracted the attention of the African American community was an all-white Little League team called Herbert Nine. This team did not exactly dazzle the world of little league sports, however. Its major attraction was the fact that the Herbert Nine was owned by none other than R. Henri Herbert, the African American political figure. The team was fully equipped with uniforms and other sports equipment.

There was no doubt numerous sand-lot teams who did not reach the sports page—or somehow were overlooked by Cooperstown, such as the team of the Colored Elks. Another popular sport among African Americans was horse racing. One of the best known jockeys during this era was John Tomkins, better known as Big John. Tomkins was a fearless horseman. He had a reputation for his breakneck escapes, especially in his younger days. He was best known for riding "Harry Bassett," a popular race horse of the day. African American Trentonians also took pride in boxer Frank McLain, "the Cuban Wonder," who at 145 pounds took on all comers.

Summary

Trenton proved to be a major focal point for African American social, political and educational growth, perhaps more so that any other northern city of its size. The struggle to achieve some measure of equality in civil rights not only made news in Trenton, but also captured the national interest. Indeed, in many ways, Trenton led the way for issues that would later command national attention. For example, the Civil Rights Act of 1875 received its first active challenge merely days after its enactment through the efforts of two Trenton African Americans, Horace Deyo and Henry Onque. The Civil Rights Act of 1875 set the stage for much needed social legislation and Trenton was in the forefront of that movement.

In the field of education, the African American community saw the passage of a school desegregation law nearly three-quarters of a century ahead of the 1954 United States Supreme Court decision in Brown vs. Board of Education. The fact that Trenton's African American community saw the need to address this issue before it was taken on in a national effort and at a time when the African American politician was just getting accustomed to the political process is nothing short of amazing.

Socially, Trenton's African American community proved to be ahead of the nation, for it was the Cuban Giants, an African American baseball team formed in Trenton, that attracted not only the attention of the African American community, but the white community as well. Often more whites attended Cuban Giants games than local African American residents.

Indeed, the Cuban Giants became so popular that season tickets were issued far in advance of the season. Much of the experience on the field is long forgotten; however, such names as Clarence Williams, Arthur Thomas, George Stoney and Jack Frye will always be remembered by old-time sports enthusiasts.

The African American community may point to politicians such as R. Henri Herbert, founder of the *Sentinel* and a leading figure in the Eclectic Club, the first social club of its kind not only in Trenton, but in the nation. It is but a small wonder that such a club boasted among its members President Ulysses S. Grant, New Jersey Secretary of State F. T. Frelinghuysen and New Jersey Governor William A. Newell. These figures openly acknowledged their membership in the Eclectic Club long before it was fashionable to do so.

In the religious realm, Trenton also proved to be advanced, for it was not long after Richard Allen founded the AME Church in Philadelphia that he came to Trenton to preach a sermon and later help to set up yet another AME Church, Mt. Zion on Perry Street. Mt. Zion helped to pave the way for other religious institutions through a strong and committed congregations.

Notwithstanding tremendous hardships, the African American community met the challenge for equal opportunity in many areas so important to all Americans today. The foresight, the struggle, the successes and the defeats were merely the foundation on which the African American community rests today. For were it not for those African Americans long forgotten, one might only speculate to what degree of progress could have been realized today.

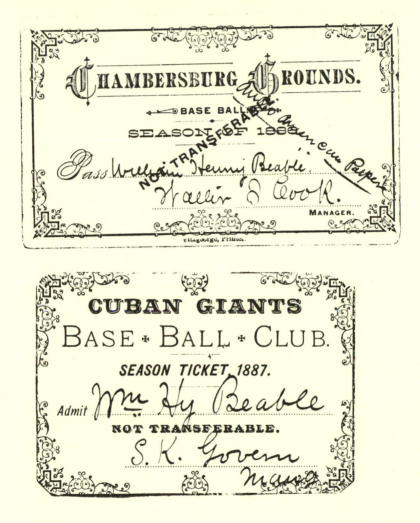